How to
Feel Younger
Longer

also by Jane Kinderlehrer

Confessions of a
Sneaky Organic Cook

How to Feel Younger Longer

by Jane Kinderlehrer

Book design by James Doddy

Rodale Press, Emmaus, Pa.

Printed in the United States of America on recycled paper,
containing a high percentage of de-inked fiber.

Library of Congress Cataloging in Publication Data
Kinderlehrer, Jane.
　How to feel younger longer.
　　1.　Aged—Care and hygiene.　2.　Middle age.
3.　Nutrition.　I.　Title.
RA777.6.K56　　613'.04'38　　74-13909
ISBN 0-87857-083-7 (Hardcover)
ISBN 0-87857-278-3 (Paperback)

　　　　8　10　9　　　　hardcover
　　6　8　10　9　7　5　paperback

Dedication

To my husband, children, and grandchildren who put the butterfly of happiness on my shoulder.

Acknowledgements

The author wishes to express her thanks to all those who have taught her that rest is rust and that real life is in love, laughter, and work.

Very special thanks to Charles Gerras for putting wings on my thoughts, to Joan Bingham for her expert and imaginative editorial help and to Irene Somishka for her considerable assistance.

Contents

Introduction

If you could rub Aladdin's lamp and be granted your wish to go back and live again, one day, one month even one year out of your past life, which age would you choose? Age 16? When your body was coming alive with changes; when every day was a threshold to some glorious future; when girls had a crush on Rudy Vallee and the boys adored Gloria Swanson; when you moved without any aching joints or shortness of breath? That was a wonderful age.

But wait. Remember how your face broke out in bumps on the eve of your 16th birthday party? Remember how you used to retire for the night with a heart full of hope and a face full of Noxema? Remember how you never knew what to do with your hands or feet, or how to handle your kid brother, your older sister or your parents who just didn't understand you at all? Remember the awful weight of the books you had to lug home from school, the homework and final exams that had you in a perpetual frenzy? Remember the awful anguish you suffered when the one you had a crush on liked your best friend? No, you wouldn't want to go through that again—not 16. It is a great age—to have behind you.

How about 21? Just as frenetic as 16 but with some of the bright illusions slightly tarnished.

How about the year of your first baby? What joy! But what panic when he ran high fevers, when he had the croup, when he had nightmares! Then came the other children, more joy, more worry. You never got enough sleep. It was a great period, but you wouldn't want to go through it again.

Then there was 40! How you dreaded 40. It meant that half your life was over and you hadn't begun to do all the things you dreamed of doing. Life begins at 40, they told you. So does the fear of vanishing youth, the advent of menopause, the loss of youthful virility, and hassles with teenage kids. No, you certainly wouldn't want to go through that again.

So, what age would you choose to return to if you could rub Aladdin's lamp and make a wish? You would probably choose the glow of 16, the vitality of 21 and the busy involvement of 40.

Just stop and think a minute about your attitude toward aging. Are you approaching 60, 65, 70? Be proud of it. Just think—you've made it. So you must be doing something right. How fortunate you are that you have been allowed to reach the time of life when you can apply your accumulated experience and wisdom to a better way of life that benefits you and those you love.

True—not everyone ages gracefully. But you can. And the very first step is to adjust your attitude. Do not dread age, but welcome it. After all, we all want to live longer. Look upon aging as a celebration of life, which is exactly what it can be if you have a healthy body, a joyful attitude and a sense of humor.

A few years ago when I addressed a group of senior citizens on the subject of "How to Look Like Marlene Dietrich When You're on Medicare," a little old lady in the front row took me to task.

"Every one of us here is at least 50 years old," she said. "We know what it's like to see old age creeping into our faces, into our hearts, into our bones. We know what it is to feel lonely, unwanted, and useless.

How does a slip of a girl like you, who is not old enough for a hot flash, have the *chutzpah* to tell us old fogeys how to stay young?"

I smiled in a Mona Lisa way. "Let me take you back a little," I said.

"Do you remember The Great Depression when engineers and architects were singing 'Brother Can You Spare a Dime?' Do you remember the soup kitchens, the bread lines and the haggard faces? Do you remember how Eddie Cantor was the bright spot of the week when he sang 'Tomatoes Are Cheaper, Potatoes Are Cheaper, Now's the Time To Fall in Love?' I remember.

"Do you remember the Charleston and the Flappers and how parents despaired about the capacity of these flippant young folk to bring up decent families? I remember; I was out there dancing up a storm. Do you remember the first World War, the great flu epidemic, the asafetida and the camphor bags we wore around our necks, the great wave of joy that swept the country when the newsboys woke us at 2 a.m. with their shouts of 'Extree! Extree! Armistice!' I'll never forget it. My sister had the flu and wouldn't take her castor oil even if it was laced with fresh orange juice.

"Do you remember gaslights and how you had to put a quarter in the meter? Do you remember the black potbellied stoves, the fragrance of fresh-baked bread, getting your hair put up in rags so you could have long corkscrew curls? I remember. We would sit around the parlor stove cracking sunflower seeds while Mom fixed our just-washed hair in rags, and Poppa would tell us stories about The Old Country.

"So, I ask you, if I remember all this, how old am I? Very soon, I too will qualify for Medicare, and if I look like a slip of a girl, it's because I feel no different today than I did when I was 16."

The little old lady who first questioned my age credentials sucked in her breath, regarded me with an air of amazement and curiosity. "How do you do it?" she breathed.

This book is my answer.

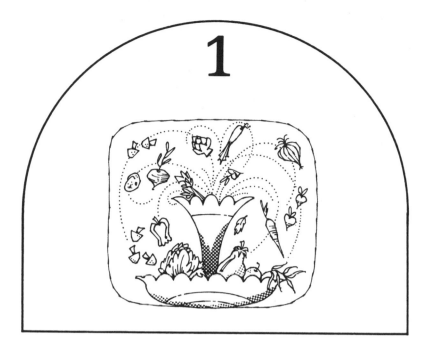

The Fountain of Youth
Is in Your Kitchen!

The poet, Robert Browning, said, "Grow old along with me—the best is yet to be." I say, "Stay young along with me and you will be equipped to enjoy the best that is yet to be"—free of the illness, despondency and despair that we see all around us among people who are over 60. Your fountain of youth originates in your kitchen.

As your body changes, you need *fewer calories* and *more nutrients*. When you learn how to plan your meals to compensate for the increased nutritional requirements that come with the increasing years, you can thumb your nose at the usual signs of old age such as dry, wrinkling skin, fatigability, irritability, forgetfulness, aching and tenderness of joints and—well, you know.

There is an old Egyptian proverb which I keep posted on my refrigerator door: "Man lives on one-fourth of what he eats. On the other three-fourths lives his physician."

This little reminder takes the edge off the munchies and makes me remember with a smile the story of Lewis Cornaro, an Italian nobleman, who lived some 400 years ago.

Maybe you've never heard of Lewis but his experience can guide you to a longer, happier life and a forever youthful figure.

Cornaro, you see, lived "high on the hog"—so high that doctors gave him up for an incurable invalid by the time he was 40. He had everything possible wrong with him and then some. His digestion was lousy. Any bug that was in the air, he would get. He was constantly plagued with aches and pains. His physician warned him that his only chance of surviving, even a few years longer, lay in changing his entire mode of living—immediately—at once.

Cornaro wanted to live. He altered his eating and drinking habits and he lived in peace and health to the ripe old age of 98.

How did he do it? He changed his regimen to one of moderation. He exercised, slept and ate at regular times—and he ate sparingly, never overloading his stomach. "In this manner," he wrote, "I conformed to the proverb which says that for a man to conserve his health he must check his appetite."

Within a year after adopting these living habits, Cornaro

was a fairly healthy man. At the age of 83 he put his formula for longevity in writing. At the age of 86 he penned a second treatise on living long. Throughout his writing he sounds a warning—do not overeat if you want to enjoy a long happy life.

"I never knew any person," Cornaro wrote, "who ate till his stomach was overburdened with much food to achieve old age. Everyone would live long, if, as they advanced in years, they lessened the quantity of their food, and ate oftener, but little at a time.

"Nor am I apt to be drowsy after meals," Cornaro wrote. "The food I take being in too small a quantity to send up any fumes to the brain. Oh, how advantageous it is to man to eat but little! Accordingly I, who know it, eat but just enough to keep body and soul together....Oh, what a difference there is between a regular and an irregular life! One gives longevity and health, the other produces diseases and untimely deaths."

There is considerable medical evidence that the aging process and nutritional depletion march in the same parade. You can halt that parade if you provide your body with *increasing* and balanced amounts of vitamins and minerals as you grow older.

How do you accomplish this? By simple arithmetic. Subtract the foods that add only empty calories; add the foods that give you important nutrients and you will multiply your chances of enjoying your latter years in the best of health.

We all know that most of the food available in the marketplace has been over-sweetened, over-salted, over-processed, loaded with additives of dubious safety and is low—very low—in the nutrients essential to health and vitality. So how can we prepare the kinds of meals and snacks that will give us the nutrients we need in order to feel younger as the years pile up?

Boost Your Protein and Minerals

Imagine that you have two boxes. One is a Pandora's box of trouble. It contains the foods on which the majority of Americans subsist—the foods that can put the wrinkles in your face, the tremor in your hand, and the crankiness in your disposition. The other box is your *Fountain of Youth*. It contains the foods that put zest and sparkle in your life. You must rid your kitchen of the troublemakers.

Let's see what's in Pandora's box! There's one trouble-making item that's found at practically every table—white bread. Almost everything of value has been removed from the grain before it goes into white bread. Because it is so deficient in life-giving values, John Lear, science editor of *The Saturday Review* aptly termed white bread "the flimsy staff of life."

It has been proven for instance that people who are deficient in the chemical element chromium are very susceptible to heart attacks. Yet, 40 percent of the chromium has been removed from the flour that goes into white bread.

Manganese is another important mineral. Studies demonstrate that when the diet of animals is deficient in manganese, they do not grow properly, or reproduce normally. When a manganese-deficient female animal does conceive and bear young, she tends to lack the quality of mother love normal to her own species, frequently rejects her own babies and refuses to suckle them. Yet, 86 percent of the manganese in whole grain is removed from the flour that goes into white bread.

Calcium is necessary to the formation of bone, Lear points out. Potassium within the cells is essential to balance the sodium outside the cells, but 60 percent of the calcium, and 77 percent of the potassium is removed from the wheat grain during the processing of the flour from which white bread is made here in America. So, remove white bread from your diet and, instead, eat wheat germ, a vitamin-mineral rich substance that is removed from white flour. You can and should add wheat germ to everything you bake and to your chopped meat dishes such as hamburgers and meat loaves. Use it as a substitute for bread crumbs in breading, use it as a dessert topping, sprinkle it over fruit salads and vegetables. But, by far the most satisfactory way to ensure yourself an adequate intake of wheat germ is to add two heaping tablespoons to hot or cold breakfast cereal. In our house, we always add the wheat germ to hot oatmeal or Wheatina. If you find wheat germ a little too coarse for a sensitive colon, whiz it in your blender for a few seconds to make it finer. I add a little wheat bran to the wheat germ,

11

because it has been shown by Dr. Denis P. Burkitt of Britain's Medical Research Council that a little bran every day will help to keep cancer of the colon away.

Protein deficiencies are common in old age. They are responsible for weariness, easy fatigue, anemia and swelling of the ankles. So watch your protein intake as carefully as you tally up your bridge score. It can double in spades your chances of being in good health to enjoy your grandchildren and great-grandchildren as well as your bridge game. A half gram of protein every day for each pound of body weight is what is recommended. So the more you weigh, the more protein you need. For example, if you weigh 130 pounds, then you need 65 grams of protein every day.

An average three-ounce portion of meat supplies about 20 grams of protein. Meat is a good source of protein, as are fish and eggs. All three are biologically complete. But organ meats such as liver, sweetbread, heart, kidney, spleen and brain are far more nutritious than muscle meats because the organ meats also contain nucleic acids, which we shall talk about later.

Ask your butcher to grind heart along with chuck or round for your hamburger mixture. Use this highly-nutritious mixture for meat loaves, meat balls, fricassees, *chow mein* dishes, rice and meat sauces, or any of your favorite recipes that call for chopped meat—*kreplach, lasagna*, stuffed cabbage, spaghetti and meat balls—you name it.

Eggs are one of the best sources of protein. There are 12

grams of protein in a boiled or a poached egg. Egg yolk is rich in lecithin, a substance which helps to emulsify not only the cholesterol in the egg yolk, but other cholesterol which your own liver has synthesized. Eggs are in your "Fountain of Youth" box. Enjoy them every day. Cheese and yogurt are fine sources of protein too. Be sure to use only the natural, unprocessed cheeses and learn how to make your own yogurt for economy's sake.

Don't overlook the high protein and low cost of legumes, grains, seeds and nuts. They give your menus infinite possibilities for delightful dishes. When you are cooking beans of any kind add wheat grains and sesame seeds to them to enhance the protein pattern. When you are cooking rice add some wheat or rye berries. Always add some soy to every recipe that calls for wheat flour and the protein value will jump. Soybeans are the legume which give you the most protein. But even soy requires a partner in the seed or grain family to make it a biologically complete protein. The story of how to enjoy a rich protein harvest from vegetable foods is beautifully explained in *Diet for a Small Planet* by Frances Moore Lappe (Ballantine). I suggest that you get a copy.

An important step you should take in order to keep young is to strive for normal weight, better a little under than over. You may have to cut down on your caloric intake to achieve this desirable goal. The very best way to do that is to eliminate all refined sugar and refined flour products from your diet. They are definitely troublemakers. Of course this includes processed cereals, bakery cakes, cookies, doughnuts, sweet buns, potato chips, pretzels, macaroni, spaghetti and so forth. You can get good whole-grain macaroni and spaghetti. You can also get some pasta products made from buckwheat flour and from artichoke flour. These are excellent foods. They provide nutrients as well as calories. The products made from white flour on the other hand contribute to all the manifestations of old age. They rob your body of needed vitamins.

Dr. John Yudkin, who wrote the book *Sweet and Dangerous,* advises, "Avoid sugar and you are less likely to become fat. One in two people who are nutritionally deficient have a heart attack, get diabetes, dental decay or duodenal ulcer. Perhaps you will also reduce your chances of getting gout, dermatitis, and some forms of cancer. In general, you will increase your life span."

Once you have eliminated refined sugar and flour from your diet, where are you going to get your carbohydrates? From fruits and juices, vegetables, wheat germ, potatoes, sweet potatoes, corn, grains, seeds and so forth. These are sources of carbohydrate which carry with them the vitamins needed for proper metabolism.

When you get up in the morning, your blood sugar is at fasting level. If you eat a breakfast that provides about 22 grams of protein, your blood sugar will rise above fasting level and will probably stay there until lunchtime. If your protein intake is less, your blood sugar will tend to return to fasting level within three hours. People who eat enough

protein at breakfast have a sense of well-being and don't feel hungry. A high protein breakfast is important if you're to stay youthful.

Stock Your Kitchen with Vitamins

Don't overlook the vitamins which help overcome signs of old age while you eat your troubles away.

All of the vitamin B's are important—particularly thiamin (B_1) sometimes called the morale vitamin because it helps to banish the blues. If you are not getting enough thiamin your appetite is poor, you tire easily, you tend to be cross, cantankerous, and impatient, you ache all over, especially in your calf muscles, and you weep at the slightest provocation, or no provocation at all. Have you experienced any of these sensations lately? To make sure that you don't, get plenty of thiamin in your diet. One way is to eat brown rice frequently. White rice won't help because the thiamin is in the outer coating of the brown rice which has been removed from the white. Other foods which supply thiamin are fish roe, fish, liver, kidneys, chicken, heart, brains, lean beef, egg yolk, sardines, desiccated liver, wheat germ and nutritional yeast. Since the body is unable to store this vitamin, it must be supplied daily. Thiamin-rich foods should never be soaked in water and should be cooked as little as possible. Get some of your thiamin from raw vegetables, sprouts and fruits—cabbage, carrots, lettuce, tomatoes, watercress, cantaloupes, bananas, avocados, dates, figs, grapes, grapefruit, apricots, apples, oranges,

15

pineapples and pears. All of these foods belong in the "Fountain of Youth" box in your kitchen.

Another very important B vitamin is riboflavin (B_2). Riboflavin aids your vision and is necessary in the oxidative processes of metabolism, which tend to slow down as the years pile up. Many of us experience burning and dryness of the eyes, lips, and feet, disorders of the cornea, scaliness around the nose, forehead and ears and don't realize that more riboflavin will help alleviate these conditions. If you feel trembly, dizzy or sluggish, this too can be a result of insufficient riboflavin which you will find plentiful in brewer's yeast, desiccated liver, eggs and soybeans. If you find that the advancing years are bringing you an increasing number of blue Mondays, perhaps you need more niacin (B_3) too. A lack of niacin can lead to nervous disorders, numbness in parts of the body, loss of memory, abdominal pain, skin eruptions and a swollen, bright-red, shiny tongue.

Niacin deficiencies are quite common because this is one of the valuable elements that's removed from grains in their refining process. It is then partially replaced in a so-called enriching process. But only one-third of the original amount is put back and this is in a synthetic form, which the body does not utilize well.

If you have those cracks around your mouth which are so typical of the aging process, if you have a shiny, beefy tongue which has failed to heal during riboflavin or niacin administration, you may need pyridoxine (B_6). Dermatitis of the ears, nose, face, chin and eyes; canker sores of the

16

mouth and tongue; and occasional nausea, vomiting and dizziness are also signs of B_6 deficiency. The lack of B_6 may lead to painful kidney stones. To prevent B_6 deficiency get plenty of brewer's yeast, wheat germ, liver, brown rice and blackstrap molasses. They all belong in your "Fountain of Youth" box.

Another one of the B vitamins that is absolutely essential in your program for feeling 39 indefinitely is B_{12}, the anti pernicious anemia vitamin found mainly in liver. B_{12} in minute quantities is considered a general tonic for adults; it helps to prevent nerve degeneration, helps recovery from skin disorders and bronchial asthma, eases bursitis and vascular disorders. Desiccated liver tablets are a dependable source.

Don't forget vitamin A for your good box. It can actually correct some of the skin changes associated with aging—the dryness and the plugging of hair and sweat follicles that give a taut-skin appearance. These are manifestations of aging that you can avoid if you increase your vitamin A intake as you grow older. Doctors have found that most people can handle 50,000 units daily without any toxic reaction. The best sources for both vitamin A and vitamin D are halibut oil or cod-liver oil. Cod-liver oil capsules taken daily tend to lubricate stiff joints and have, in one member of my family, relieved the swelling and pain of arthritic fingers. Be sure to put cod-liver oil capsules in your "Fountain of Youth" box.

If you are becoming stooped and losing stature as you

grow older, you may need more vitamin D. Dr. Thomas Mochella of the University of Pennsylvania, who did intensive vitamin-balance studies on a group of elderly people, says that vitamin D should be administered to all people who are deprived of sunlight for prolonged periods of time, especially the elderly person who suffers a fracture and is confined to a bed in a room without sunlight. Cod-liver oil capsules will supply you with just the right ratio of vitamin D and vitamin A.

When you plan your stay-younger-longer campaign, don't, for heaven sakes, overlook your increasing need for calcium, vitamin C and vitamin E.

Many of the signs of aging are not inevitable at all, but simply warnings. For example, if you feel that your heartbeat is a little irregular; that your bones ache; that you don't sleep so soundly as you used to; that you can't hold a cup of tea with steady hands; you can't climb a flight of stairs without getting winded; your teeth are brittle and more subject to cavaties; you get dizzy spells; lose your temper easily; sometimes feel faint and nauseous, your body may be warning you that your blood is low in calcium as a result of calcium being low in your diet. Because all these symptoms are related to low levels of calcium, try adding bone meal powder and brewer's yeast (which is the same as nutritional yeast) to tomato juice for a ten o'clock pick-up. Indulge in snacks like this and you won't be tempted to reach for a sweet.

Increasing your vitamin C intake with each birthday is

18

perhaps one of the best insurance policies against the wear and tear of the years. The older you are, you see, the more DDT, lead, food additives and other toxic substances have accumulated in your system. Vitamin C is needed by the liver for the detoxification process. But vitamin C is not stored in your body. It must be taken frequently because, as you grow older, it is called upon to perform more and more jobs. If you find yourself bruising easily, if you have spongy, bleeding gums and loosening teeth, or pain in your bones, you probably need to take more vitamin C.

Swedish women, known for their luscious complexions, use certain natural foods to stay young and beautiful. Swedish beauty secret number one is rose hips, perhaps the richest source of natural vitamin C. "Rose hips made into a tea is the Swedish fountain of youth," says Dr. Paavo O. Airola in *Health Secrets from Europe* (Parker, 1970).

Dr. Airola also noted that, "The adrenal glands secrete over 20 steroid hormones which are directly involved in the business of keeping your vital bodily processes operating at high efficiency. A decrease in the output of these hormones usually begins in late middle years and is responsible for the symptoms of aging. Russian researchers have demonstrated that substantial daily doses of vitamin C have a rejuvenating, stimulating effect on the glandular activity and hence the vital hormones are once more produced at a higher level similar to those produced by younger people."

Dr. Airola states that, "The healthy function of sex glands is directly related to general health and to the

19

appearance of youth. A Japanese doctor, M. Higuchi, has demonstrated that there is a relationship between vitamin C levels and the hormone production of the reproductive glands. In addition to vitamin C, vitamin E (which is sold, labeled as the sex vitamin, in automatic dispensers in Sweden) plays an important role in the efficient activity of these glands. Prostatic fluid, which nourishes the sperm and keeps them alive, is extremely rich in vitamin C. A deficiency of vitamin C and vitamin E can slow down the hormone production of sex glands and consequently lead to premature aging."

Dr. Airola summed up his findings by saying, "If there ever has been a real miracle substance, vitamin C is it. It has so many universal applications that it is impossible to find a condition of ill health, disease, or diminished well-being which vitamin C would not affect favorably, very often with a miraculous healing effect. Since old age is often associated with various conditions of diminished health, it stands to reason that vitamin C should be *rejuvenating tonic number one for everyone over 40 years of age.*"

Vitamin C is also a highly-potent antitoxic agent that protects the body from many kinds of poisonous substances. Since growing old is often associated with sluggish metabolism and an accumulation of poisonous substances, it is easy to understand how large doses of vitamin C can have a rejuvenating effect.

Perhaps the most vital function of vitamin C is keeping collagen, the cellular cement, healthy. Collagen is the elastic matter that holds all the tissues together, tissues of the muscles, organs and tendons as well as tissues of the skin. The most visible symptoms of aging are in the skin. It loses its youthful, tight appearance and fresh color. Then, wrinkles appear on the face, neck and hands. These aging symptoms are largely due to the unhealthy state of collagen. When tissues are healthy, they are strong and elastic like new rubber bands; the skin is tight and has the look of youth. When collagen loses its tensile strength, it becomes like an old worn-out girdle, it allows muscles to sag and the tissues of the layer just beneath the skin to become weak. The skin becomes wrinkled.

Hardening of the arteries and atherosclerosis are two diseases of premature aging. Many doctors believe that you are as old as your arteries. Dr. Boris Sokoloff, director of the Southern Bio-Research Institute in Florida, reported in the *Journal of the American Geriatric Society,* December, 1966, that there is widespread medical evidence that ascorbic acid (vitamin C) is the key factor in averting atherosclerosis and that this form of heart disease, which leads to heart attacks, may be a vitamin C deficiency disease.

Can Vitamin E Help You Live to Be 150?

Dr. Olga Lepeshinskaya, one of the Russian scientists engaged in research on longevity, says in her book, *Life, Age and Longevity,* that the *normal* life span of the human being should be not less than *150 years.* Anyone who feels old before reaching 100, she says, is suffering from premature old age which, like other diseases, can be largely prevented by sound, simple, natural nutrition.

At the Institute of Biochemistry of the Russian Academy of Science, experiments with vitamin E have shown that it has an enormously beneficial effect on people suffering from the diseases of old age, specifically when it is taken in combination with vitamin A. The rejuvenating properties of these vitamins have a direct effect on the sex glands. They also strengthen the ability of the tissues to absorb oxygen, restore impaired circulation in blood vessels, especially in the small capillaries, and help to restore the normal permeability of the blood vessels.

It is well known that Russians eat enormous quantities of sunflower seeds and use unrefined, cold-pressed sunflower oil. Sunflower oil is rich in vitamin E and essential fatty acids. Sunflower seeds are also an excellent source of complete protein, B-vitamins and minerals. Other good sources of vitamin E are wheat germ oil, wheat germ, and unrefined corn oil and soy oil.

Proper Elimination

Constipation is a problem of many people over 40 and it is a condition which hastens the aging process. It can be a simple matter to cure constipation—if you do not resort to laxatives and cathartics. I cannot emphasize this strongly enough. The remedies frequently taken for a slight irregularity can cause chronic constipation by damaging the mucous membranes and the secretory cells. Mineral oil also

robs the body of its fat-soluble vitamins.

The first thing you do to avoid constipation is eliminate the devitalized foods—the refined flours and starches from your diet. These foods are seriously altered. They lead to constipation because all of their stimulating elements have been removed.

Refined sugars, whether they are made from cane or beet, are in the class of devitalized foods. Sugar irritates the mucous membranes. The constipating effect of an overabundance of these foods is produced by drawing so much of the intestinal fluid to them, for their solution and absorption, that the bowel contents are deprived of sufficient moisture to keep them soft and pliable.

The average person eats little or no fruit, except perhaps during the summer. But it is during the colder months, when the diet is heavy and consists mainly of starches and protein, that fruits are needed most. They improve not only the quality and circulation of the blood, but every function of the body, not the least of which is waste elimination.

One of the easiest ways to relieve constipation is to increase your consumption of water. The average person consumes far too little. The tissues and cells of the body cannot function normally, they cannot absorb nourishment nor discard their waste, and they are not so responsive to nerve stimulation when they are denied a sufficient amount of diluting, dissolving water. All functions are reduced when the intake of water is low.

If you tend to forget to drink water, here's a good way to remember. Place six or eight pennies on the windowsill or counter by the kitchen sink. Each time you drink a glass of water, transfer a penny from one side of the windowsill to the other until you have moved all the pennies during the course of one day. This is very effective.

A very old remedy for constipation, one that has been used by some of the world's most beautiful people, is a drink made from the juice of half a lemon in a cup of warm water taken upon arising in the morning. This should be taken 30 minutes before breakfast in order to get the full benefits. No sugar, please. This drink is working, not as a food but as a cleaning and purifying agent.

Another extremely effective regulator is apple cider vinegar—2 teaspoons, once or twice daily, taken in a glass of water just before meals.

Eating a green salad every day is another way to insure regularity. In the spring, our grandmothers tried dandelion, poke salad, mustard greens, and any number of wild plants for "cleaning the winter body." Any greens are a welcome addition to the diet—chicory, romaine, endive, raw spinach, Chinese celery and cabbage. Greens contain bulk or fiber which becomes highly-magnetized in its passage through the intestines, drawing from the body used-up tissues and cell wastes.

Molasses, the unsulphured kind, is a pleasant way to help your body rid itself of toxins—so is raw honey. But perhaps one of the best regulators is yogurt. Yogurt establishes the friendly bacteria which sweep the body clean. Don't use the commercial fruited yogurts. They have too much sugar. Get plain yogurt and add your own fruit—apples, pears, oranges. Throw in a handful of sunflower seeds and you have a dessert that's better than cheese cake.

Exercise is very important, too. Walking outdoors is one of the greatest body regulators. Take deep breaths of fresh air while you walk.

An excellent exercise to promote natural elimination is the body-raising pose. It strengthens the abdominal muscles. Lie flat on the floor. Lace your fingers behind your head, supporting the upper part of your neck and lower part of your head. Inhale deeply, and at the same time raise your head, shoulders and legs off the floor, keeping your knees straight. Hold this position, along with your breath, for a few seconds, then exhale and slowly return to a flat position. Do this twice the first day. Gradually work up to six times, increasing by one more each day.

Irregularity of meal hours is another cause of constipation. The digestive organs become adjusted to supplying their secretions at specific hours. When a meal is delayed a few hours, or advanced a few hours, the rhythmic movements of the intestines and colon are disturbed and constipation may follow.

Chew Your Food

Many older people may eat well-balanced meals and

still fail to get proper nourishment because they fail to chew food sufficiently.

Your food must feed your body all of its nutrients. This is accomplished by proper digestion. If you lack digestive enzymes, proper digestion is impossible because the enzymes extract vital life-giving vitamins, minerals, proteins, and amino acids from the food. Good enzyme power has its foundation in good chewing. This means that you must chew and chew well if you expect enzymes to do a good job.

Reducing Blood Sugar

There are three natural foods—blueberry leaf tea, Jerusalem artichoke and the lupine bean—which have been found to lower blood sugar without any dangerous consequences.

Diabetics need a good supply of vitamin B$_6$ and magnesium because diabetes takes the magnesium out of your body before it gets a chance to perform its important jobs. Adelle Davis advises, "Any person with diabetes or a family history of the disease would be wise to take at least 10 mg. of B$_6$ and 500 mg. of magnesium daily." B$_6$ is present, along with all the rest of the B complex, in *wheat germ, yeast and liver. Dolomite* is an excellent source of *magnesium*. Diabetics also need adequate lecithin to help them metabolize fats.

Many of the nondescript pains suffered by the diabetic can be prevented to a large extent by taking brewer's yeast

with every meal. Calcium is lost by the diabetic to such an extent that osteoporosis is common in diabetics. This is a sure indication that bone meal should be included with the diabetic's food supplements.

Nucleic Acids

There is another facet to growing older which must be considered. As you age, so do your nucleic acids, which are your genetic blueprint. Their patterns become less distinct and the replication of cells is consequently less accurate. Such aging in the liver reduces the secretion of bile. A diminished supply of bile increases the likelihood of infection and decreases absorption of the fat-soluble vitamins, A, D and E. As the liver becomes less efficient, there is less utilization and more excretion of these valuable vitamins.

In order to compensate for this effect and slow up the slow down, make it a point to increase your intake of foods which are rich in nucleic acids—brewer's yeast, organ meats, liver, heart, lung, sweetbreads, kidney, fish— especially sardines, and fish roe. At the same time you should increase your vitamin A intake because this vitamin helps to incorporate the nucleic acids in the liver.

In one multidisciplinary study reported at a Washington meeting, a group of healthy, elderly men were followed over a 12-year period by investigators at the National Institute of Health in Bethesda, Maryland and the Philadelphia Geriatric Center.

Of the 47 men in the study (average age 71.5 years) 23 were still alive after 12 years and 19 were available for follow-up examinations. These follow-up examinations revealed that to enjoy your latter years to the hilt, it helps if you are smart. It was found that those who had survived the 12-year period of the study were those who had scored significantly higher on intelligence tests taken at the beginning of the study.

It is also interesting that those who survived showed no significant decline in test performance over the years. For the original group of 47 men survival was associated with the retention of intellectual vigor and capacities. It sure helps if you have an up-beat attitude.

Does wealth mean longevity? It helps if you consider yourself rich. As far as financial status was concerned, the study revealed that it was not so much what they had but how they managed on what they had that differentiated between the two groups. For instance, 80 percent of the short lived and only 30 percent of those who achieved a longer life ranked themselves as having just "enough to get along" or "can't make ends meet." As the Talmudist said, "Who is rich? He who is content with what he has."

Physical Symptoms, Too, Cast a Prophetic Shadow

In a report of the medical and physiological factors affecting mortality, Leslie S. Libow, M.D., noted that some of the 47 subjects showed "multi-system, asymptomatic evidence of arteriosclerosis (hardening of the arteries).

28

FOUNTAIN OF YOUTH IS IN YOUR KITCHEN

These subjects later had a significantly higher mortality rate than non-affected subjects."

Dr. Libow pointed out that even in the healthy group with low blood pressure, death occurred more frequently in those subjects who had the highest systolic pressures at the beginning of the study. (Systolic blood pressure is the blood pressure when the heart muscle is contracted. Blood pressure is generally expressed by two numbers, as 120/80, the first representing the systolic, and the second the diastolic pressure.)

Cigarette smoking and calcification of both carotid arteries (those which supply the head and neck) were also correlated to mortality at the five-year follow-up examination in this study.

Some other factors found to be associated with a lower mortality rate at the ten-year follow-up examination were: maximum breathing capacity, evening diastolic blood pressure, and mean arterial blood pressure.

Who then has the best chance to achieve a happy old age? Anyone who is enjoying life, is intellectually interesting and interested, keeps in good health and doesn't use tobacco.

It Adds Up to Health

The big question mark is—what makes one man enjoy life while his brother does not? What is it that contributes to sexual vigor? What helps make a good marital adjustment? Why does one person retain intellectual vigor while another becomes senile?

Your earning power is certainly enhanced when you have ambition, drive and energy, all qualities which are the natural outgrowth of buoyant good health.

What about learning? Certainly intellectual curiosity, ability to concentrate, and desire to learn are enhanced by good health.

Mental alertness, a good memory, a lively interest in the world around you are all symptomatic of good health. And good health, of course, is the dividend you earn as a result of good nutrition and wholesome living.

You have only to explore the benefits of nutrition and discover a new, youthful you.

Correct your eating habits and you will add years to your life and life to your years. You can be among those who light up a room with your inner glow long after you qualify for Medicare.

George Bernard Shaw once said that youth is wasted on the young. But, when you have the wisdom of age and the vigor of youth, you have an unbeatable combination. The point is you don't have to go to Florida or to Shangri-la or even to the Catskills to find this unbeatable combination—this glorious fountain of youth. Once you've learned what to add and what to subtract from your market basket, you'll find the Fountain of Youth *in your own kitchen.*

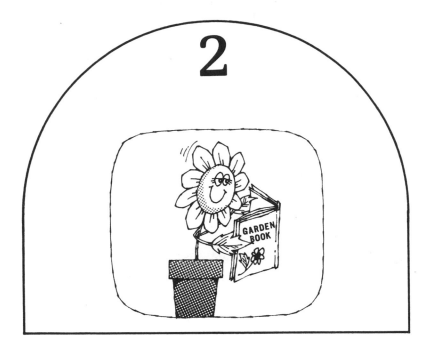

Busy Hands
Are Happy Hands

You would never guess it to look at her, but Rose L. is the life of every party. Why? It isn't that she has the eye-catching appeal of a 25-year-old, though at 80, she still has a charming aura of femininity. You wouldn't call her glamorous either. She has little sense of style, and she doesn't know Charles of the Ritz from Estee Lauder. In fact, she puts nothing on her face but a smile, but Rose can tell a story like Sholom Aleichem. She can take the news of the day, view it with considerable wit and wind up with a delightful anecdote. She is interested in people. That's why Rose is the life of every party.

When I asked her how she maintained her youthful enthusiasm and zest for living, she said, "Each day, first thing in the morning, I slip into an active mind. You see, the mind matures as the body grows old. Age and experience add up to a kind of wisdom you cannot learn at school. Today, at 80, I am as healthy, merry, and happy as if I were 39—like you!" she winked.

I learned from Rose that graduating from the "in" crowd doesn't mean slipping into the rocking chair to watch the passing scene. It's a wonderful time to learn new skills and delve into areas which have long piqued your curiosity. It's a time to *live it up,* and if you do, research studies indicate you will actually *live longer.*

Recently, a 63-year-old woman called the New School for Social Research in her area and asked if she was too old for the Speed-Reading Workshop. The registrar told her that there were even older students. The woman then asked if she could register for the karate course too, and the answer was yes.

This woman was doing more than widening her horizons. She was taking out survival and anti-senility insurance. She was incorporating into her life at least one of the two factors which were found, in a recent study, to be accurate predictors of which healthy senior citizens will survive while others succumb to old age. This study, conducted over an 11-year period by the National Institute of Mental Health, revealed that the most significant of the more than 600 variables evaluated turned out to be "the organization of one's daily behavior." The second most important indicator is the presence or absence of chronic cigarette smoking. The study was published in the *Journal of the American Geriatric Society* in April, 1973.

I don't know if our friend who was interested in furthering her education is a smoker. But a preoccupation with needlework can certainly keep one's hands so busy that there's not much opportunity nor inclination to reach for the tar and nicotine.

In fact, the brain, not the body, may be the pacemaker in the process of aging. "The older brain," says Dr. Leslie S. Libow, Chief of Geriatric Medicine at City Hospital Center, Elmhurst, New York, "is far from being diminished in capacity. It is actually a strong, experienced, intelligent and well-nourished organ."

The amount of blood which reaches the brain is one measure of the vigor of that organ. And, other things being equal, the brain is as well supplied with blood and as vigorous in old age as it is in youth. It has been shown by Dastur, Sokolof and Associates that the cerebral blood flow of 70-year-old people is no different from that of 20-year-olds as long as arteriosclerosis has not dominated the picture. (HEW publication #936, U.S. Government Printing Office, Washington, D.C.)

Even people with significantly decreased cerebral blood flow need not withdraw from the mainstream of life and new adventure. The powers of memory for distant events remain largely intact. So do the powers for abstract reasoning, arithmetical and intellectual skills.

This study gives us something new and interesting to

think about. In the past, an organized, busy day has hardly been considered a health indicator. Yet it was found that *"the greater the organization, complexity and variability of a day's behavior, the greater the survival."* This information should encourage us to pursue many new and exciting directions. It should also force us to rethink our treatment of the older people we know.

With the best of intentions, many times we try to relieve our older folks of the necessity for planning their own lives. Are we doing them a favor or shortening their lives when we advise them to move out of their big homes, give up their gardens and move to a small efficiency apartment so they are relieved of the difficulties of maintaining an establishment?

The question of enforced retirement should also be reviewed. Since it may be a long time before changes are made in this area, if you are facing retirement you will probably add happy years to your life if you take the time to develop new interests.

Abstaining from smoking is an important factor in keeping your mind young. Tobacco narrows the blood vessels and restricts the flow of blood to the brain, which is why smoking often causes dizziness and blurred vision. So sooner or later smoking will affect your mind. Millions of heavy smokers have found the motivation to quit and thus enhanced their chances for a happy old age. One gentleman who had smoked three packs a day, told me he was able to quit by substituting vitamin C lozenges for cigarettes

whenever he got the urge for nicotine.

Others have found the Smoke-Enders Program valuable in the battle to escape from the nicotine ball and chain. As a reformed smoker myself, I can tell you from personal experience that the rewards of freeing yourself from the shackles of tobacco are well worth any withdrawal pains. Do not let the fear of putting on weight deter you from making every effort to kick the habit. If you snack on such things as celery sticks, carrot strips and raw turnips instead of sweets, you probably won't put on weight. On the contrary, you will improve your digestion and your health. But even if you should put on some weight, do not be dismayed. I gained five pounds while I was fighting the nicotine habit. But, I knew that if I had the willpower to quit smoking, I also had the willpower to lose the extra pounds and I did.

You will find after you quit smoking that you have more pep and a more optimistic outlook on life.

Indulge in some form of physical activity. Join a walking club, a hiking club or a bird-watching group. Play badminton or tennis, go skating or go bike-riding if that's your thing.

Make yourself useful, find some way to render an important service to your community. One of the most rewarding areas is service to a hospital. The Gray Ladies at our local hospital, most of them in their 60's and 70's, tell me that being a Gray Lady has taken the "blue" out of their lives.

Service of this type is not limited to the ladies. Many men of retirement age are finding ways in which they can make a meaningful contribution in a hospital environment. I have seen some of these gentlemen sparkle as they swap tall tales with patients. Some of the men help to feed patients. And some whittle animal figurines to entertain children in the pediatrics ward. All of them, because they are rendering a service which is needed and appreciated, straighten up and walk like they were ten feet tall. They may not realize it, but they are also warding off senility.

Another venture not to be overlooked, which can bring you a great deal of pleasure and outdoor exercise too, is backyard gardening. Of course, make it organic. You will enjoy the thrill of picking and eating vegetables grown in your own chemical-free soil.

If you enjoy gardening and would like to supplement your income at the same time, consider the Green Thumb workers, a little-known organization which provides jobs for the elderly, most of whom receive social security checks that are scarcely big enough to keep them going.

Green Thumb workers, whose average age is 69, receive $1.85 an hour for two or three days work each week and earn a maximum of $1,630 yearly. Green Thumb operates nationally in 24 states including Puerto Rico. It employs some 3,414 men and 290 women on a budget of nine million dollars supplied by the U.S. Department of Labor.

The projects which Green Thumb workers have tackled this year include making and repairing picnic tables in local parks, repairing volunteer fire company houses, painting

rooms at community hospitals, creating roadside rest areas, draining a mosquito-infested swamp, planting trees, clearing underbrush in parks, working in day-care centers and visiting the sick and retarded. Green Thumb serves a dual purpose for its workers. It supplements incomes but more important it provides its workers with a feeling of being needed. Try gardening;many people are turning to the land as a hobby as well as a means of self-support. For information on Green Thumb, contact the U.S. Department of Labor.

If you have no backyard or land of your own, why not start a community garden? It's being done all over North America, from California to Maine, through groups from churches to park councils to banks. An excellent booklet called *Gardens for All—a Guide to a Greener, Happier Community* published in Charlotte, Vermont, can be your guide and inspiration. The programs described in this booklet have liberated thousands of people of all ages from the limits of apartment walls to the nearly limitless advantages of backyard fruit and vegetable growing. People have many reasons for vegetable gardening—enjoyment, relaxation, exercise, recreation, a sense of accomplishment, new friends, savings and profit and, of course, an abundance of better tasting, healthier foods.

Last summer my family and I did some gardening in a community plot made available to us by Rodale Organic Gardens. We found that gardening produces not only gorgeous vegetables, but a feeling of oneness with God and man, a chance for mental and physical relaxation, a sense of

37

sharing with fellow gardeners, and the satisfaction that comes with accomplishment. The garden was our focal point for weekends of family dig-ins and we became especially close on our common ground.

No matter where you live, there must be a piece of land which is begging for the plough. In Burlington, Vermont, aspiring gardeners found church property, sites around factories or offices, city parks, vacant lots and open rural land outside the city which was laying idle. These tracts of land were made available for small fees or for free. People got together who like to garden but just didn't have access to enough land. Dianne Young and the *Garden Way* editors who describe the venture say, "A little effort and cooperation between civic leaders, organized groups and associations, people in government and area land owners, brought together people and the soil and resulted in a happy and beneficial reality for all."

Whether you garden or not, make sure that you always have some kind of productive work to do. It is important to a happy retirement even if you have no need for extra funds. Back in 1953, Harold R. Hall told a meeting of the Gerontological Society in San Francisco, "Most retirees report that relying on hobbies alone for retirement does not bring full satisfaction." One retired man said, "For me hobbies are like dessert, I have to have some meat and potatoes..."

And above all, don't think that you're too old to explore a new field of knowledge. Education is moving from the

campus to the living room via television, records or cassettes. Avail yourself of all of them.

And don't be afraid to tackle a tough, challenging job like accepting the chairmanship of a committee. If you have expertise in a certain field by all means put it to use. The good you can do is immeasurable. Mr. Hall suggests that you should become involved in some work that brings a degree of pressure and tension with it. This may strike you as strange but, as Mr. Hall points out, "The circumstance seems to be that executives have become so used to business pressure that the need for a minimum of tension remains in the system after they leave their companies."

Get yourself involved in community efforts in behalf of your peers. One of the best community efforts which has come to my attention is a senior activity center called Little House, in Menlo Park, California. It provides a meeting place for senior citizens, opportunities to find companionship, to discover new interests or pursue former interests in educational, recreational and craft activities; and, at the same time, they contribute to the welfare of the community.

A hot meal is served every day, and doubly enjoyed because it is companionable. The many arts and crafts classes are helping the participants to discover talents they never knew they had. Language and discussion groups stimulate their minds; lectures and musical presentations give them an opportunity to share their know-how and experience the lovely flush that comes with applause.

Recreation and social events bring them together in happy fellowship, and community service projects give them that wonderful feeling of being an active and important part of the community. Just look at this wide range of activities Little House offers: weaving, dressmaking, china painting, oil painting, Japanese brush painting, rug making, mosaics, ceramics, flower arranging, knitting, novelty crafts and sewing, lapidary (cutting, polishing and engraving precious stones), woodworking, and gardening. And that's not all. These busy, happy folk also participate in square dancing, bridge, and folk dancing. Did you ever have it so good?

This Menlo Park center could be a model for other communities. A booklet describing the center is available from the Superintendent of Documents, U.S. Government Printing Office, Washington, D.C. 20402. It is called *An Activity Center for Senior Citizens,* Case Study #3 by Cutter, Russel, and Stetler.

Many people think that old age and senility march in the same parade. This is not so. Senility is avoidable and often reversible. It is the *fear* of senility which haunts the lives of many old people. Because they forget a name or an address or an occasion now and then, lots of people over 65 fear that they are becoming senile. "Only one in six people over 65 is actually senile," says Douglas S. Looney, (*National Observer,* March 31, 1973.)

"Frankly, I believe that people bring senility upon themselves," comments Mrs. Muriel Oberleder, Assistant Professor of Psychiatry at Albert Einstein College of

Medicine, New York City.

There is general agreement among the experts on this point. Says Dr. James Folsom of the Veterans Administration in Washington, D.C., "I think some people have been born senile. They've never had an original thought. They don't grab life; they let life grab them." He offers some excellent advice: "Be active. It is far better to slip on the ice and break your hip than to slip on a rug and break your hip. Too often older people are seated in a comfortable chair rather than being up doing something."

Bela Kaufman, granddaughter of the great storyteller Sholom Aleichem, tells an amusing tale of a woman in her late seventies, who every morning—winter and summer—takes a dip in the Atlantic ocean. "Aren't you afraid?" Bela asked her on one occasion.

"Why should I be afraid?" the intrepid swimmer replied. "I would much rather die when I'm swimming, which I love, than die while I'm doing dishes, which I hate." She certainly has a point there.

For the senior citizen who wants very much to live long and joyfully, Mr. Looney suggests a "thinking man's diet." "Eat properly," he says, "vitamins may help. Get adequate sleep but avoid constant dozing. Be interested; be smart. Learn new skills. Think in terms of second and third careers." Colonel Sanders started his chicken business when he was 66. He is now a robust, active 83-year-old who just completed a 30,000 mile, five-week trip around the world. Fame and fortune and true fulfillment came after the age of

60 for Picasso, Casals, Winston Churchill, George Bernard Shaw, Grandma Moses, and many others. How about you?

As for my husband and me, we are only a few years from Medicare, but we still dance a mean hora, polka, and tango. At a recent square dance, we outdistanced and outmaneuvered most of the dancers who were friends of our kids.

At my lectures, people frequently corner me and ask, "Confidentially, how old are you?" So I tell them, "Confidentially, I am 61 going on 16." There is nothing which I was able to do at 16 which I cannot do better today.

Don't give up things in the name of "I'm getting old and forgetful." This is a big step toward senility. If you go roller skating today, you can go roller skating tomorrow. If you ride a bike or play tennis today, you can do it tomorrow too.

Do give up smoking. Yes. And do improve your nutrition. Then you will have the vim, the vigor and the will to "Live It Up and Live Longer."

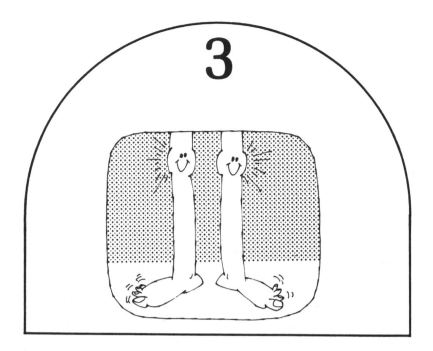

March into Medicare on Healthy Feet

I've never heard it said that you are as old as your feet. But, if your feet hurt, you sure don't feel young.

Foot problems seem to increase with age, according to two podiatrists who have made a study of feet that have been walking around for a half century or more. It seems that just about the time you're looking forward to Social Security and travel, trouble with your feet is apt to trample your plans.

Rare indeed is the person who marches into Medicare with happy feet, judging by the findings of Dr. B. Rakow, Chief of Podiatry Service at Coney Island Hospital and Dr. Sandor A. Friedman, Chief of the Chronic Disease Unit. They realized the prevalence of foot problems when, over a three year period, they examined 201 patients admitted to the hospital's Chronic Disease Unit (*Geriatrics*, May, 1969). These patients were not in the hospital because of their pedal problems. They were older people who needed nursing or custodial care. And yet, when the shoes came off, most of the patients were suffering silently with either ingrown toenails, thickened toenails, corns or calluses and excessively dry skin.

These are all conditions which are potentially dangerous, especially when they're associated with another condition which the doctors found in 161 of the 201 patients: no pulse in the pedal extremities. Your doctor calls it arterio insufficiency. A foot without a pulse is vulnerable to a host of problems. It has no defense. Any break in the skin may lead to infection or gangrene because the increased requirement for blood flow cannot be met. The transportation system has broken down.

Poor circulation is a condition to guard against no matter what your age. Cramps in your feet or legs at night, a tendency to have cold feet or feet that hurt when you walk are yellow caution lights warning of trouble ahead. It is foolhardy to ignore these problems. They indicate poor circulation and poor circulation can trigger many other problems, some of them very serious.

Chances are, you won't have any of these problems if you make certain before you get to the rocking chair stage that you always have a pulse beating in your foot. In other words keep your peripheral circulation percolating.

When it comes to peripheral circulation, your best

friend can be alphatocopherol (vitamin E), the vitamin all but lost in modern food processing.

The effectiveness of vitamin E in problems involving peripheral circulation has been demonstrated many times at the Shute Institute in Canada. Dr. Wilfrid Shute, in his book *Vitamin E for Ailing and Healthy Hearts* (Pyramid House) describes the case of a 61-year-old woman, a known diabetic for 33 years, who was brought to the Institute with gangrene in the heel of her right foot. It had begun as a small ulcer some ten months previously. If this woman had presented herself to the usual doctor or surgeon, she would have been scheduled for surgery at once, to have her leg amputated above the knee. Medical textbooks and journals maintain that diabetic gangrene involving the heel cannot be conservatively treated. Dr. Shute feels differently. By the end of four and one-half months on a dose of 1,200 units of alphatocopherol daily, not only did his patient's insulin requirements drop from 35 to 10 units daily, but her gangrenous heel showed definite signs of healing.

Usually, in the process of healing, epithelial tissue tends to contract, and the wound becomes tender as it shrinks. But with vitamin E treatment, the tissue healed without contracture, the heel wound showed no shrinking and no tenderness and, best of all, the patient was able to walk in perfect comfort on her own two legs with just a rubber pad in her shoe.

How does vitamin E work to help your feet? It helps to dilate the arteries and so it strengthens the action of the heart. The result is it improves the flow of blood. So vitamin E is not just a treatment for a specific ailment. It improves your general health. One of the dividends of this improved health is better circulation to your extremeties.

One of the most common clinical manifestations of pulseless feet induced by a deficient blood supply is called intermittent claudication. Claudication means limping or lameness. It's called intermittent because in the beginning it only hurts when you walk.

This condition can become very painful though it sneaks up on you gradually. You might feel just a slight pain when you walk. Not an extreme pain—just a slight annoyance that you dismiss as nothing to be concerned about. You might feel it in your foot or thigh, but the calf of the leg is the most common site of discomfort. The pain gradually intensifies until you find yourself making excuses for not walking. Occasionally you may feel a sharp constricting pain, like a muscular cramp, in one or both legs, sometimes accompanied by severe fatigue.

In heavy smokers, intermittent claudication is frequently the first symptom of Buerger's disease. When this disease gets you the pains are not limited to times of exercise, but bother you even when you are at rest. You are frequently awakened by severe cramping that can involve both calves and feet. You feel the need to get up and walk or at least hang your feet over the edge of the bed to get some relief.

The good news is that many of these conditions can be

avoided with vitamin E, says Dr. Shute. Vitamin E increases the speed of the opening up of collateral circulation and the extent to which it opens.

Exercise is another simple and effective way to improve circulation to the feet and legs but it is often overlooked in our motorized society. While you are walking, the leg muscles actually serve as a sort of a "second heart" because they move the blood upward against gravity. The late Dr. Paul Dudley White, famous heart specialist, said in a syndicated newspaper article (February 3, 1969) that leg muscle exercise through walking is one of the best ways to keep the veins clear and prevent blood clots. He recommended a one-hour walk every day.

That's fine. But if your legs hurt, or if you have corns or calluses, walking can be torture and you and all your good intentions may end up in a rocking chair.

Again, our old friend vitamin E can come to your aid. Vitamin E not only provides more blood but more oxygen to the legs and feet, making possible the restoration or maintenance of normalcy.

Not everyone suffers with intermittent claudication or Buerger's disease. We hope you don't. But, if you are old enough to dandle your grandchildren on your knee, chances are that unless you've always guarded your health with proper nutrition, you're having some kind of trouble with your feet. If you're young enough and healthy enough to have feet that feel great, you couldn't do yourself a better favor than to keep your feet that way. In either case, vitamin

E and sensible exercise to improve your circulation, plus well-fitting shoes that let your toes move and your feet breathe, will help you become one of those few people who "march into Medicare on happy feet."

When you have healthy feet you can indulge in one of the best forms of exercise—walking.

When a *New York Times* reporter asked Mr. Roebuck of Sears and Roebuck, on his 90th birthday, to what he attributed his good health and longevity, he replied; "All I want you to tell your readers is that on his 90th birthday, Mr. Roebuck took his usual walk in Central Park."

From my own experience, I can say that there's nothing like a nice brisk walk to take the wrinkle out of your brow.

Walking is a great exercise which requires no investment in fancy equipment, it's companionable, and it can open up a whole new world of pleasure for you. It will also help to keep your midriff lean, it will greatly improve your morale and your cardiovascular health. Try it. You'll like it.

I realize that this is not sensational news. You've known it all along. Even your doctor has probably told you to get out and walk, and you've meant to. But have you?

If it's motivation you need, consider that a good brisk walk not only lightens your heart, it strengthens every beat of it. In fact, a program of walking can help your heart as much as more strenuous forms of exercise like jogging. And walking, like jogging, is aerobic, that is it makes more oxygen available to the body.

This was determined by Michael L. Pollock and his

associates at the department of physical education, Wake Forest University in Winston-Salem, North Carolina. To find the effects of walking on the cardiovascular function and body composition of middle-aged men, Pollock chose 16 healthy but sedentary men between the ages of 40 and 56 to participate in the investigation (*Journal of Applied Physiology,* January, 1971). These men were tested on a treadmill, their oxygen-intake capacity was measured, their heart-rate response to a standard treadmill walk and a one-mile walk were measured and body composition measures were determined.

What were the results? You'll be surprised. In two significant areas a fast walk can be more effective than a slow jog. First, walking can improve your body proportions more quickly. Second, it can have a more aerobic effect on your cardiovascular system.

Anything which increases the oxygen capacity of the heart and lungs can improve your cardiovascular health and actually spell the difference between life and death by heart attack.

The walking group, Pollock and collaborators found, displayed a significant increase in maximal oxygen-intake capacity. Some subjects showed an increase as high as 28 percent.

This is such an important dividend that everyone of us should be eager to get out and walk a few miles to achieve it. Imagine! As much as 28 percent more oxygen for your heart! Remember, it is lack of oxygen which usually triggers a heart attack. If your heart is getting 28 percent more, then the risk of a heart attack from oxygen starvation is 28 percent less. This increased oxygen supply is better protection against a heart attack than all the pills in your doctor's little black bag.

And that's not all. The lungs benefit too. Pollock found that pulmonary circulation increased by 15 percent. This improvement in your wind gives you increased stamina and permits longer walks without exertion.

Besides this considerable improvement in the cardiovascular picture, the walking group had a lower diastolic blood pressure, a general improvement in physique, a reduction in total body weight and in overall fat. They cut a much better figure in their swimming trunks as their chests expanded and their waistlines diminished.

As these gentlemen began to taste the joys of walking, the gentlemen who were sitting it out suffered a loss in chest expansion and their pot bellies increased. They looked years older than the walking members of the study, and they felt it too.

Add to these considerable dividends the fact that walking can extend your life by giving you the use of what has been termed "a second heart."

Nature, you see, doesn't put all her eggs in one basket. She has provided your heart with an auxiliary system to ease the load of pushing some 72,000 quarts of blood every 24 hours, over nearly 100,000 miles of circulatory byways. The muscles in your feet, calves, thighs, buttocks and abdomen actually give your heart a great big assist. As they work, they rhythmically contract and expand, squeezing the veins and forcing the blood along. It's nature helping the heart to move the blood to the upper part of the body in spite of the pull of gravity.

This whole system is made more efficient when you walk. Walking makes the muscles below the waist do their part. Without their help there can be many unhappy consequences such as varicose veins or phlebitis. The heart must work much harder when it gets no assist from your leg muscles. It must move that blood in order to deliver essential nutrients to all your tissues.

Because of this phenomenon, walking is now recognized as an important therapy in the treatment of heart patients. Doctors have learned that walking is the best way to make the lower muscles take over their share of the work and relieve the damaged heart. Even a short walk improves circulation and causes the heart little effort. In *The Magic of Walking* (Simon and Schuster, New York) authors Aaron Sussman and Ruth Goode say that "People whose heart rate and blood pressure are high will find that a regimen of regular walking—not necessarily far or fast—helps bring the heart rate and blood pressure down to normal levels."

Many of us are old enough to remember the days when taking a little walk was a popular activity for a Sunday afternoon. The town's main boulevard would be alive with Sunday walkers. It was a gay, pleasant activity with people window shopping and stopping to greet friends. This kind of promenading, unfortunately, is now out of style. Few people walk just for the fun of it; hardly anyone walks to work or even to the corner drugstore. What is the result? More people are getting heart disease, digestive and elimination problems, and flabby muscles than ever before. Certainly a good share of the blame for the rotten shape we're in is due to physical inactivity.

Literally every part of the human body is called upon to perform when you walk. Your lungs dilate with fresh, invigorating air. Your muscles stretch and turn with every step. Your limbs, neck, rib cage, pelvis, spine and buttocks, all move in a coordinated rhythm. Your joints automatically "oil" themselves to make the going smooth and your senses perk up.

In spite of the fact that you feel little strain when you walk, walking does demand real physical effort. The muscles that you use take in such a wide area and the effort involved is so widely distributed that no one set of muscles runs the risk of being overtaxed.

A Beneficial Weariness

A four-mile an hour gait is top speed for the average walker. But one hour of continuous walking at three miles an hour is still a vigorous and stimulating workout.

Let your arms go when you're walking. Without the natural swing of the arms coordinating with each step, the body's rhythm and balance are disturbed. The right arm moves with the left foot, and the left arm moves with the right foot. At any easy walking gait the hands ought to dangle loosely, swinging in and out like pendulums.

You may feel some fatigue after a brisk three-mile walk. But it is a pleasurable kind of fatigue. Dr. Paul Dudley White, heart specialist, in a report to the American Medical Association, termed this kind of fatigue after exercise "remarkably enjoyable." If you don't experience it, he said, you are "missing something invaluable. A pleasant fatigue of the muscles has time and again given me mental repose, peaceful sleep, and a sense of equanimity."

As far as losing weight on your walking regimen, don't expect miracles. Remember, you are converting fat or flab into muscle and muscle weighs more than fat. It is, of course, far more attractive and useful to you. While it isn't the fastest route to a bikini figure, over the long haul, walking can do wonders for your figure. While the act of walking doesn't burn a great many calories, walking briskly does stimulate your metabolism which lights a fire under those unwanted calories.

If you can possibly find a companion or two or three to join you in your daily walks, this can make the adventure much more enjoyable and will encourage you to stick-to-it.

If, however, you must walk alone, then enjoy your own company and the scenery around you. Study the faces of the people you pass, observe the sky, trees and birds. Incidentally, it is good for the eyes to scan the distant horizon. It exercises eye muscles that you rarely use in your close daily work at home or in the office.

J. I. Rodale (who was a great walker) used to figure out plots for plays and stories on his daily walks. When he found himself in a tight spot, he would go out for a walk and then his thoughts would begin to flow beautifully.

It takes an extra push to start any new program. But once you have done something three times, it tends to become a habit.

There are several ways you can get started. Organize a walking group or join a hiking club.

Park your car one mile from the office and walk. Keep your business shoes in the office and walk in the most comfortable shoes you own. If you must carry papers and books home with you, try a knapsack slung over your back rather than a briefcase that can weigh heavily on your arm.

Instead of taking the family for a ride on Sunday afternoon, take them for a nice walk.

Head for a pleasant woodsy area and combine your walk with nature study; look for wild flowers or edible plants.

Give your morale a great big boost; give your heart a daily treatment; give your midriff a lean look. Get out and walk. You'll like it.

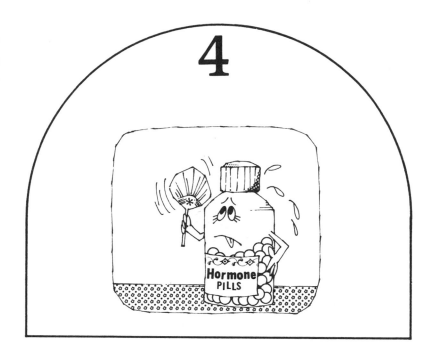

Cool Hot Flashes— without Hormones

Sooner or later, it happens to every woman. And it always comes as something of a shock—that first hot flash. I remember it well. It happened in the middle of opening night. We were doing *Milk and Honey* and I was playing Mrs. Levy—the Molly Picon role. I had just finished singing the first bar of my big number—"Hymie, for seven years I've been good..."—and it hit me! My face and neck seemed to catch fire. Of course, I didn't know what it was that hit me, I thought it was Hymie, from the other side of the clouds, trying to communicate with me using lightning rods as the medium. When I finished the song the applause was so wild it made me dizzy. That's what I thought. I got the same feeling the next night in the middle of the "Chin up" number, and the day after that in the middle of lunch. So I had to cancel Hymie out as the source of all this heat.

I wasn't aware of what was happening to my hormones until several weeks later when my sister was visiting. We were getting things ready for dinner and in the process I was taking off one piece of clothing after anotner.

"Are you doing a striptease or having a hot flash?" my sister asked.

"Hot flash?" I reeled. "But it can't be—I'm much too young!"

"You may feel young, kiddo, but you're old enough to be all finished with that nonsense. Some women start in their thirties, some in their forties and you're in your fifties." Who but a sister can shock you with the reality of your own age?

So, it was time to turn the page and start on the third chapter of my life. What would it be like? Would it be distressing? Would it be painful? Would it be the end of something wonderful?

I learned that menopause is not so much an ending as a beginning—the beginning of a new maturity, a new gentleness, a new sense of freedom. I learned that life gets better in some subtle fashion. I learned that you can sail through the menopausal years without tears and without estrogen. There's been so much ballyhoo about synthetic estrogens being the answer to staying "feminine forever" that many a woman approaches the menopause wondering if she should take estrogens, with all the risky side effects. And many a woman thinks the alternative is to endure the hot flashes, the dizziness, the brittle bones, the dry skin, the loss of the feminine mystique, and all the other over-emphasized consequences of going through this perfectly natural change in a woman's life.

I remember that my doctor once remarked that what a woman needs most at the time of menopause is not synthetic estrogens, but an appreciative smile which says, "You're still okay, baby."

Menopause is, after all, just another milestone that you have reached on your road through life. Congratulations. Just as every girl one day "becomes a woman" and begins to ovulate and menstruate in order that she might have babies of her own, every woman, usually somewhere between the ages of 40 and 55, graduates from the businesss of producing babies. Nature, in her wisdom, closes up the shop. You cease to ovulate and cease to menstruate.

The little girl approaches, with wonder and excitement, the prospect of becoming a woman, the advent of the second act in her life. And every woman can approach menopause with anticipation and high expectations. It is, after all, the third act in the drama of being a woman. It can be the best act of all—if you are nutritionally prepared for it.

You can be feminine forever—without synthetic estrogens. The pathway to this kind of healthy, carefree menopause starts, not in the drugstore, not on the psychiatrist's couch, not even in the doctor's office. It starts in your kitchen. The age to prepare for a happy menopause is whatever age you are today. Because anything which contributes to your good health now will pave the way for a smooth opening on act three.

You must remember that the changes going on inside as your body shifts gears create a stress condition. To meet this stress, your body demands certain nutrients. If these demands are met, no strike—no problems. If they are not met—lots of problems, lots of misery.

A difficult menopause can turn a charming, confident woman into a shrew. It can lead to depression, bitter quarrels, unhappy wives and miserable husbands. It can even lead to divorce.

But what causes a difficult menopause? The medical profession terms the menopause a "deficiency stage"—a deprivation of vital substances. These vital substances are hormones.

Acting on the premise that all these changes going on in your body are due to the shutdown in the estrogen department, many physicians immediately prescribe the little estrogen pill and you wait for a miracle. True, the effects sometimes seem miraculous, but are they? There are certain psychological effects which accompany hormone therapy.

Even if a woman has no hang-up at all on the consequences of taking the pill, hormone therapy alone will not improve her emotional state because it was not hormone deficiency that made her tense, irritable or depressed.

If you conducted a poll of pre-menopausal women and asked them point blank, "What one thing do you dread most

about the menopause?" You can bet that nine out of ten would say, "the end of the feminine mystique."

Is the estrogen treatment more myth than miracle? Are the problems we associate with menopause merely problems associated with growing older? Professor H. Kaiser, of Augsburg, Germany says, "Science has come to realize that most hormone glands change their function only slightly in old age, and that causal connection between aging and hormone production is just a fallacy. The coveted hormone inoculation cannot stop the process of aging."

Some doctors see the situation as simply ridiculous. Women come in asking for the youth pill, Dr. Sherwin A. Kaufman, of New York University Medical Center, told the American College of Obstetricians and Gynecologists at a conference held in Washington in 1967. "They say 'check my estrogen level.' From what they've read, they think it's as simple as driving into a gasoline station and having their oil checked."

Many women, who are not aware of the limitations of the estrogens or the possible consequences expect the estrogen pills to solve—not just the problems of menopause, but all the problems of middle age which they equate with menopause. These problems include: hot flashes and insomnia which the hormones usually alleviate, (so will vitamin E—without any side effects); brittle bones and blood vessels, and heart disease—which the hormones tend to stabilize for a while (but which can be alleviated by a diet rich in calcium, magnesium, phosphorus, other vital trace minerals, and vitamins). Women expect the estrogen to keep their skin from wrinkling—which it won't. A high protein diet, plus the unsaturated fatty acids, lecithin and vitamins A and D can help keep your skin youthful and elastic. They expect to prevent sagging breasts and a flagging libido for which the hormones will do nothing, according to the testimony of the gynecologists who expressed their views at the Washington Scientific Meeting.

Vitamin E, on the other hand, has been known to work magic in both these areas.

There is one thing which the estrogens do, however, which is important to sex without pain. They do prevent the drying up of the vaginal mucosa. At the menopause, a woman does not secrete the fluid which before menopause was the testament of her desire. This lack is easily remedied, however. Any lubricating cream, vaseline, A & D ointment, or even wheat germ oil, applied locally before retiring is simpler and safer than estrogen therapy.

You need never suffer loss of sexual desire or suffer bedroom fatigue, if you know what to do in the kitchen to keep your glands forever young. You can, in fact, actually cool your hot flashes with vitamin E, an ingredient which has been stripped from your bread, flour, cake and macaroni, and which processing removes from practically all your food. If you are eating a diet of refined and processed foods, your menopause could indeed be a misery because you just can't get a decent amount of this vitamin from such a diet.

By clever substitution of live foods for devitalized foods, by a subtle change of snacks, you can actually provide the elements needed by your bones, by your skin, and by your glands.

There is one phenomenon which is frequently overlooked and which is the key to menopause without misery. At the time of menopause the ovaries cease producing eggs and decrease their estrogen output. True. But what is generally not known is that the activity of the adrenals and other glands is stepped up to compensate for this loss. If your adrenals are well nourished and therefore not worn out, they are ready and eager to take up the torch. But if your adrenals are already overworked and undernourished, you may experience some of these symptoms of adrenal exhaustion: hypertension, nervousness and tremor, abnormal perspiration, dry mouth, flushing, chills. Do these symptoms sound familiar to you?

What do your glands need to be healthy whether you are 30 or 60? They need specific nutrients. Make sure your diet is rich in all the B vitamins. Some of your best sources are wheat germ, brewer's yeast, liver, whole unrefined grains, nuts, beans and brown rice. (Never use white rice. It has been stripped of its important B vitamins—especially B_1 which is absolutely essential to your morale. This one vitamin can help transform a mean and miserable woman into a pleasant, charming one.)

An undersupply of thyroid hormone results in fatigue, loss of interest in sex and a tendency to gain weight rapidly on few calories—many of the symptoms women associate with the menopause.

Iodine is necessary for a healthy thyroid. Since vitamin E greatly increases iodine absorption and the production of hormones by an underactive thyroid gland, they should be taken together. Try some wheat germ oil in a glass of tomato juice and spike it with a generous dash of kelp. A high protein diet speeds the activity of a sluggish thyroid by supplying the amino acid tyrosine from which the thyroid hormone is made.

While many women are taking the estrogen pill and simply postponing the day of reckoning, more and more women are discovering vitamin E.

This therapy is gradually gaining favor among physicians. The use of vitamin E to relieve the symptoms of menopause is not new. But since no pharmaceutical house has a proprietary interest in any vitamin, vitamin E as a treatment for menopause just never made the kind of dramatic headlines accorded to the estrogens.

But many studies in medical literature demonstrate its dramatic effect. Back in 1950, Dr. N. R. Kavinoky described in the *Annals of Western Medicine and Surgery,* the treatment of 92 patients with vitamin E in doses ranging from only 10 to 25 milligrams daily. Thirty-seven women who had complained of hot flashes were delighted at the relief they obtained. Sixteen who had suffered from backaches were immensely relieved. Of 34 who had had very heavy menstrual flow, 16 showed tremendous

improvement with a greatly diminished flow.

Encouraged by these results, Dr. Kavinoky tried larger doses in another group of women and reported even better results. High blood pressure and vague muscle pains were relieved. Half the patients reported relief from fatigue and nervousness. More than 50 patients reported that they were sleeping much better and all of them reported relief from dizzy spells, heart palpitations and shortness of breath. Some women felt the improvement in only two weeks. Others took two or three months.

Back in 1952, Dr. Henry A. Gozan reported some great improvements in menopausal patients using much higher dosages of vitamin E. The report of his treatment appeared in *The New York State Journal of Medicine* (May 15, 1952). He treated 35 menopausal patients with 300 units of vitamin E daily, in conjunction with good nutrition. Nineteen were improved or completely relieved within two to four weeks.

It was pointed out by R. Fuhr, *et al,* in the *Annals of the New York Academy of Science* (1949), that during the menopause the need for vitamin E soars 10 to 50 times over the previous requirement. Hot flashes and night sweats frequently disappear when 50 to 500 units of vitamin E are taken daily.

Vitamin E is not a once-and-done therapy. It must be continued. H. C. McClaren pointed out in the *British Medical Journal* (2, 1378, 1949) that symptoms quickly recur when the vitamin is stopped. If estrogen is given, the need for vitamin E increases still further, Dr. Fuhr pointed out.

While alphatocopherol (vitamin E) can be effectively combined with almost any other treatment, there are three commonly used drugs with which it is incompatible. In the book, *Vitamin E for Ailing and Healthy Hearts,* by Wilfrid E. Shute, M.D., with Harald J. Taub (Pyramid House, New York, 1970), we learn that inorganic iron, mineral oil and the female sex hormone, estrogen, interfere with the metabolism of vitamin E. Iron leaches it out, and if iron must be given for anemia, it should be kept from coming into direct contact with the vitamin E. Take all your vitamin E in one dose and all your iron 8 to 12 hours later.

Vegetable oils dissolve alphatocopherol but readily release it in the body, while mineral oil dissolves it but doesn't readily release it.

In her book, *Let's Get Well,* Adelle Davis warns against using cold creams made from mineral oil. Not only estrogen but adrenal hormones and vitamins A, D, E, and K dissolve in mineral oil, from which many cold creams are made. Mineral oil is absorbed through the skin when creams containing it are used. The net effect is the sacrifice of vital hormones and vitamins. Avoid mineral oil in all forms. Look for creams with a base of avocado oil or other vegetable and animal fats.

Is there any danger of overdosing with vitamin E? According to Dr. Shute, who has done extensive work with vitamin E for almost 40 years, there is no one who cannot safely take 50 units of vitamin E daily. Because vitamin E dissolves clots and therefore promotes healthy circulation of the blood, those who are suffering with hypertension or high blood pressure should start their vitamin E at a low dosage of about 50 I. U.'s per day and gradually increase.

But there is never any danger of overdosage if you obtain your vitamin E from wheat germ oil. Researchers are not sure what substances in wheat germ oil have such a miraculous effect on the health of the reproductive system, but in some experiments a synthetic vitamin E was not able to duplicate the results obtained by wheat germ oil.

Dr. Paavo Airola suggests in his book, *Sex and Nutrition* (Information Incorporated, 1970), that one or two teaspoons of wheat germ oil each day, or the equivalent in wheat germ oil capsules, will provide a good supply of vitamin E. He also recommends two or three tablespoons of fresh raw wheat germ each day sprinkled over cereals or mixed with juices or milk. Other food sources of vitamin E are rice germ oil, sunflower seed oil, safflower oil, peanut oil, raw walnuts, filberts, almonds and some green vegetables. But there are other substances besides vitamin E which are important to a happy menopause.

If you are suffering symptoms such as nervousness, irritability, insomnia, headaches and depression, you may attribute them to the menopausal syndrome. In a way, you're right. But these symptoms may occur because you are seriously deficient in calcium. Calcium is not well absorbed when estrogen decreases. This lack of calcium may also be why you suffer a pain in the back. It is why some people develop a stoop in their upper backs. Sometimes this is called osteoporosis, or porous bones. Many people date their pain in the back from the onset of the change of life. This is because the supply of estrogen in the female system diminishes with menopause. This leads to demineralization of the bone structure.

Porous bones, however, are not an inevitable part of the menopause—not if your nutrition is meeting the excessive demands which the stress of menopause places on your body's machinery.

The most logical treatment for osteoporosis is calcium supplementation, according to one of America's top authorities, G. Donald Whedon, M.D., director of the National Institute of Arthritis and Rheumatic Diseases. In October 1967, in a memorial lecture to the medical faculty of the University of Ottawa, Dr. Whedon observed that, "Regardless of its multiple causes—osteoporosis is characterized by overactive resorption of bone, brought about by an insufficiency of calcium (whether due to a dietary deficiency, malabsorption, or excessive urinary loss) which stimulates parathyroid secretion." (The parathyroid is the gland whose hormone triggers the release of calcium from the bones.)

Calcium supplementation is effective only when you are getting phosphorous, magnesium, and vitamin D to permit the structure of the bone to absorb the calcium. A natural and effective calcium supplement is bone meal which contains not only calcium but phosphorous, magnesium and many important trace minerals. Many bone meal formulas

which include vitamins A and D are available.

If you aren't getting sufficient protein in your diet, you're practically asking for menopausal problems. Dr. J. D. Walters proved this in an experiment reported in the *Journal of Applied Nutrition* (Volume 10, 1957) by substituting good nutrition for artificially administered hormones. Of the 726 patients on hormone therapy who were examined, 81 were vegetarians, and 56 of them were willing to accept temporary additions of meats to their diets. Estrogen levels, as well as the androgen and ketosteroid hormone levels, rose in 65 percent of the subjects when they began to eat meat. Those vegetarians who refused meat were advised to cut down on cereals and cooked vegetables and to concentrate on non-hydrogenated oils, raw nuts and sunflower seeds. When they consumed one to four ounces of nuts and seeds daily, they showed a rapid rise in their hormone levels. Pumpkin, squash and sunflower seeds were rated most effective.

Because studies indicate that nutrition can effect a change in the hormone balance, and that the body will take care of itself if given the proper nutrition, the American Academy of Nutrition in recognition of the important role played by diet in menopause has set up these guidelines as a preventive against hormone imbalances:

1. Serve foods in their original state whenever possible (raw rather than cooked).

2. Cook foods at low heat to preserve nutrients.

3. Cook vegetables in a minimum amount of water, for

as short a time as possible and save the water for other cooking (it's rich in important minerals).

4. Eat plenty of protein (meat, fish and eggs).
5. Avoid sugar and sweetened foods.
6. Consider nutrients not calories in planning your diet.

If you follow this regime and make sure you get plenty of vitamin E and calcium, you too, can one day say to your family as I did, "Look! No hot flashes, no estrogens, no tears!"

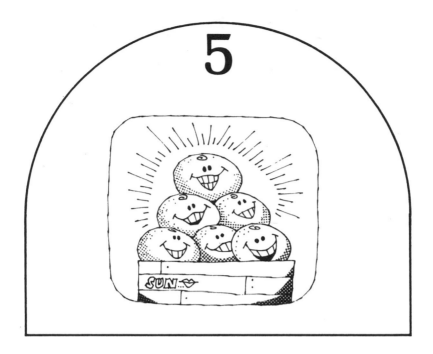

Are You Afraid to Smile?

At a backyard barbecue party last summer, I noticed that three people at our table of eight passed up the corn-on-the-cob which our hostess, Sally, had prepared so lovingly. The corn was so sweet and so tender I enthusiastically ate every kernel.

"You must have good gums," one of the non-corn eaters remarked with a small touch of envy.

My eyebrows went up. "Why gums? I'm still chewing with my teeth."

"Yeah," he said. "I have good teeth too. But they're loose in the moorings. I'd give my eye teeth to be able to eat corn-on-the-cob and that's probably what I'd do if I tried. Let me tell you something," he said, "you're a rarity. My periodontist told me that 85 percent of everyone over 40 has gum problems that cause loosening of the teeth."

So if you, like me, are over 40 and have no sign of periodontal disorder, you must be a rarity too. And you must be doing something right. That's good, because periodontal disease is something we can live very nicely without.

It begins with inflamed gums, as too many of our contemporaries know, and it leads not only to pain and expense but often to tooth extractions. The teeth you lose may have been perfectly good molars or cuspids to which you have long given tender loving care. But if the condition of your gums is bad, there isn't any way to anchor them in your mouth.

We tend to think of teeth as being cemented to the jawbone. They are not. They are anchored in their sockets, strongly supported by protein fibers of collagen, one of the most important parts of the periodontal membrane. When these collagen fibers are destroyed, the teeth are no longer supported properly. They become loose and eventually are lost. That's why so many people over 40 have beautiful, white, uniform teeth which grin at them from a drinking glass every night.

Periodontal problems are a dental tragedy. How do you avoid them? Ask your dentist and he will tell you that thorough tooth and mouth hygiene and regular visits to the dentist for removal of plaque formation are of prime importance. That's fine. But it isn't enough. Unless your

70

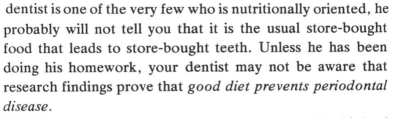

dentist is one of the very few who is nutritionally oriented, he probably will not tell you that it is the usual store-bought food that leads to store-bought teeth. Unless he has been doing his homework, your dentist may not be aware that research findings prove that *good diet prevents periodontal disease*.

When you think of healthy teeth you probably think of calcium, phosphorus, magnesium, fluorine, and the other minerals which contribute to the strength of the bone. Who would ever think of vitamin B_1 in connection with the oral tissues? Yet, when Dr. M. J. Walsh analyzed 16 nutritive factors in the diets of 254 adults suffering periodontal disease, he found thiamin (B_1) to be the most deficient nutrient. The second was, believe it or not, vitamin C. Calcium was third (*Journal of Periodontics,* October 1952).

The funny thing about a B_1 deficiency is that it sneaks up on you when you're not looking. It doesn't cause specific oral lesions. But if your gums are peculiarly sensitive to hot or cold or to acidic foods, then you should suspect a vitamin B_1 deficiency. Dr. Lowell M. Peterson, D.D.S., of San Francisco, points out, in *The Journal of Applied Nutrition* (Winter, 1972), that patients with a deficiency of thiamin tend to have sensitive oral tissues.

Thiamin is considered the "morale" vitamin, the vitamin which stimulates a lagging appetite and nourishes your nerves. Actually, if your dentist were doing his homework, he could sense a B_1 deficiency just by the way you react in the dental chair. A low pain threshold which is peculiar to many dental patients can be indicative of thiamin (B₁) deficiency, wrote J. L. E. Bock in *The U.S. Armed Forces Medical Journal,* March, 1953. The loss of thiamin from the nerves is one of the major factors in the production of pain. But replacement of free thiamin to the injured and diseased nerves relieves pain and restores proper functioning.

Thiamin is a most important vitamin in your program to stay young as long as you live. It is vital to the oxidation process that goes on with every beat of your heart and in every single cell of your body. More thiamin is needed when you shovel snow, or jog, or vacuum the rugs, or dance a hora. If you smoke, drink alcoholic beverages, use antibiotics and other drugs, you can say goodbye to some of your vitamin B₁ stores.

It is important for you to be aware of the many ways in which you are using up your B₁ and to continually replenish your supply. You get thiamin in brown rice, in wheat germ, in brewer's yeast, and in desiccated liver. Sunflower seeds are also a good source of thiamin.

Important as thiamin is, it isn't the only member of the B family which helps to protect your oral tissues. Deficiency of niacin (vitamin B₃) can cause perfectly good teeth to loosen because of a wasting away of the sockets in which they are imbedded. Niacin deficiency, which in extreme cases leads to pellagra, is much more common than is recognized. According to the Vitamin Information Bureau, an independent research group, "It is as likely to occur in

favored debutantes as in chronic alcoholics and with freakish diets as well as in wasting disease."

Since lesions in the mouth are signs of advanced B vitamin deficiencies, it would be good "save-your-teeth insurance" to check periodically for deficiencies. If your gums are tender, if you have a swollen, bright-red tongue, if you are overly anxious or feel numb in various parts of your body, you should suspect a niacin deficiency and immediately increase your supplementation in this area. Here again, brewer's yeast, desiccated liver and sunflower seeds are good sources. Don't waste your teeth on high-sugared, oversalted snacks. Instead, put a variety of seeds in your snack dishes. You will be taking a giant step toward keeping your teeth in your head and not on a nightstand.

Another member of the B family which can come to the aid of your teeth and gums is pantothenic acid. Pantothenic acid patrols the gum line. When laboratory animals were depleted of pantothenic acid in experiments, they developed gum abnormalities leading to the death of gum tissue. The destructive aspects of a deficiency in pantothenic acid resemble those of a niacin deficiency, but there is no warning inflammatory response. There is no swelling and no leukocytic infiltration. In other words, it's a sneak attack. But one which offers a most fertile field for rampant infection.

If you are one of the millions of people who awaken every morning with stiff jaws after a night of grinding your teeth, you're not only manifesting a deficiency in pantothenic acid, but the habit itself contributes to gum problems.

Bruxism, the scientific name for tooth grinding, is more than just an unpleasant habit which disturbs your spouse. It is a prominent cause of tooth loss and gum recession, both of which result from the loosening of the tooth in its socket, induced by frequent grinding.

Three out of every 20 children are contributing to paying off the orthodontist's new swimming pool as they gnash their molars out of line. But adults too, in fact, one out of every 20, are adding to the nocturnal cacophony and their own gum problems.

Don't let anyone tell you that your tooth grinding is due to mental illness or emotional disturbances. Psychological tests on matched groups of grinders and non-grinders recruited among University of Chicago students gave no indication that the grinders were any more emotionally disturbed than the non-grinders (*University of Chicago News Release,* February 13, 1968).

In fact, a report in the December, 1970 *Dental Survey* revealed that bruxism is a *nutritional* problem that can be greatly ameliorated with increased dosages of both calcium and pantothenic acid (the anti-stress vitamin).

Why should these two nutrients be involved in a phenomenon that disturbs the slumbers of millions of people every night? Besides being vital to the strength of the bones, calcium is used by the nerves and was pinpointed by 1970

Nobel Prize winner, Sir Bernard Katz, as the key requirement for transportation of impulses along the nerves from one part of the body to another. Lack of calcium will cause cramps or convulsions. A convulsion is a violent involuntary series of contractions of the muscles. What is bruxism? An involuntary movement of the muscles of the mouth bringing the teeth together in a grinding movement.

The role of calcium in helping to alleviate bruxism is understandable, but what part is played by pantothenic acid? This fraction of the vitamin B family is essential to proper function of the adrenal glands. When these glands don't produce important hormones you are vulnerable to stress. Tooth grinding is just one manifestation of stress.

A good supply of pantothenic acid may be just what you need in order to cope with your stresses and avoid gum problems. Okay, so how do you get pantothenic acid into your diet? It is important to remember that this member of the B family is quickly destroyed by heat. Consequently it is largely lost from milk which has been pasteurized. There is none left in canned milk, prepared formulas or canned baby foods. This might be one reason why three out of every twenty children are grinding their teeth while they sleep and setting the stage for gum problems.

Adults too are being cheated of pantothenic acid when they rely on the usual refined, overprocessed diet. This vitamin is lost in refining or any kind of heat treatment and it is not replaced by the so-called "enrichment" farce. Nutritional yeast, desiccated liver, sunflower and sesame seeds are excellent sources of pantothenic acid. Bruxists should grind sesame or sunflower seeds between their teeth when they are awake and spare their families sleepless nights.

Besides the vitamin B family, other nutrients are of vital importance to the health of your gums and teeth. Calcium is involved at the very root of the problem. It is true that periodontal disease starts when the gums become inflamed. The gums swell away from the teeth and small open pockets are formed between the teeth and the gums. Bacteria collects in these pockets and the toxins produced by the bacteria eat away the fine filaments that connect the teeth to the gums and bone. The pocket deepens, the foundations of the teeth weaken, and eventually the walls come tumbling down. The teeth are lost.

But what causes the gums to become inflamed? First the bone is affected, then comes the gum inflammation which aggravates the disease, according to Dr. Per Henrickson and Dr. Lennart Crook of the Pathology Department of Cornell University (*New York Department of Health Bulletin,* May 20, 1968).

How can you prevent this kind of bone destruction? High calcium-intake is very important.

The average American does not get nearly enough calcium. At least 1,100 milligrams daily are required to compensate for normal losses. This is 35 percent higher than the average dietary intake!

The other nutrients which are vitally important in your

campaign to keep your gums healthy are vitamin C and the bioflavonoids. Those fine filaments that connect the teeth to the gums and bone need collagen, which maintains the integrity and stability of your body's connective tissues. And vitamin C and the bioflavonoids are absolutely essential for the building of collagen.

Sore, bleeding gums is one of the classic symptoms of scurvy, which results from a lack of vitamin C. At the first sign of bleeding gums or pink toothbrush, you will be wise indeed to greatly increase both your vitamin C and your bioflavonoid intake.

Ample protein is also vital to healthy gums. Dr. C. B. Holmes and Dr. D. Kollier compared the diet history of a group of Seventh Day Adventists' children with a similar group of other children. The Adventist group ate only one-fourth the amount of animal protein and one-half the amount of sweets. They had fewer cavities, but a greater degree of periodontal disease (*Journal of Periodontology,* March-April, 1966).

There's a lesson here for those who would heed it, and encouragement too. Gum problems can be avoided completely when your nutrition is excellent. But even if the problem has begun, the case is not hopeless. When my friend Nettie went to the dentist and was told that her gums were so bad they would have to be cut down to the bone, she asked for time. Then she went on a megavitamin program for a year. She took vitamin C with bioflavonoids—3,000 milligrams daily; bone meal—9 tablets daily; desiccated liver—9 tablets daily; nutritional yeast—3 tablespoons taken as a broth daily; vitamin E—600 I.U.'s daily. She also took an all-purpose vitamin mineral supplement daily.

Her gums showed a continual improvement and, to her dentist's amazement, they were pronounced perfect at the end of the year.

So you see, determined use of supplements can help you redeem the health of the tissues in your mouth before you join the legions of those who can no longer enjoy corn-on-the-cob in company.

6

Don't Reach
for That Antacid!

Let's face it, one of the most distressing problems of the over-40-going-on-60 crowd is indigestion, bloating and distress after eating. Many of us are making a big mistake in the way we handle it.

For instance, we had a very nice dinner party last Saturday night. Since my specialty is "making people healthy when they're not looking," everything on the menu was designed to build health and encourage good digestion. There were no, "no-no's." And yet, two of my guests expressed their compliments in a rather uncomplimentary manner. They slipped antacid pills into their mouths.

"I have a nervous stomach," one said. "I can't live without my antacid pills."

"My problem is raw fruits and vegetables," the other said. "I love them, but they blow me up like a zeppelin. That's why I take an antacid after every big dinner."

They were making a big mistake; so are you if you rely on antacids, and so are the great majority of people, young and old, in our country.

An inquiring tv reporter recently queried the passing throng with the question, "What do you take for indigestion?"

Sixteen out of 20 said, "I take an antacid."

One girl who appeared to be in her late teens said, "I live on Alka-Seltzer."

Judging from this assay of the public's churning stomachs, distress after eating appears to be endemic in this country and every Mary, Mabel, Max and Joe suffers with chronic indigestion—heartburn, bloating, belching, cramps and gas pains. The sad thing about it is that practically all of them attribute this distress to acid stomach and reach for one of the 575 different antacid tablets, liquids, powders, lozenges, gums or pills on the market, hoping for a quick ticket to relief.

All of the millions of people who spend a whopping 200 million dollars every year on antacid preparations are making a big mistake.

Actually, what practically everyone needs, especially those over 40 years old, is not less acid but more hydrochloric acid! "Many millions who think they are suffering from overacidity are not!" says Dr. William Ellis.

"They are suffering from underacidity. (The symptoms are the same.) Every time they reach for an antacid medication, they are easing the distress, but compounding the problem!" The older you are the less efficiently you manufacture this essential acid. Many people over 40 have no acid production at all.

"In fact," Dr. Ellis told me "If I had but one thing to practice medicine with, it would be hydrochloric acid! [the acid of the stomach.] Acid in your stomach is absolutely necessary—to break down proteins and minerals, to aid digestion, as well as to destroy harmful bacteria," Dr. Ellis maintains. "The medium of the stomach is acid. If your stomach isn't acidic, you're in big trouble."

"The proper use of hydrochloric acid could save more lives than all the drugs in the pharmacopeia," another authority on HCL, Dr. Herman Dorn of Miller Pharmacal, West Chicago, told me. There is much more illness attributed to over-alkalinity than to hyperacidity. The trouble is the symptoms are always the same."

Hydrochloric acid is a truly amazing substance. It is, says Dr. D. C. Jarvis, author of *Arthritis and Folk Medicine*, (Holt, Rinehart and Winston), about three million times more acid than the blood.

A sufficiency of HCL permits the stomach to open at the right time, thus you have digestion without distress. An insufficiency of HCL can be the first step to a whole complex of serious problems—gastritis, gastric carcinoma, pernicious anemia. This is how it works:

As soon as you swallow your food, it encounters the gastric juice, a complex fluid secreted by glands in the lining of the stomach. Gastric juice consists of water, inorganic salts, hydrochloric acid, mucin and enzymes. The presence of hydrochloric acid in one of the body fluids is a remarkable phenomenon that has intrigued physiologists for many generations. Though it's three million times more acidic than the blood, hydrochloric acid still does not damage a healthy stomach. Why? There is a thick, tough, flaky mucus found in the gastric juice which is secreted by cells that line the stomach. This mucus adheres to the cells that secrete it and protects them from the corrosive action of the hydrochloric acid as well as from abrasive action of various solid substances that may be swallowed.

If your digestion is normal you are continually secreting some digestive juice. By far the greatest amount, however, is secreted after meals. Actually you start secreting gastric juice in increased volume as soon as you see, smell or taste your food. The more you anticipate the pleasures associated with eating, the more gastric juice you will secrete. But if you have little appetite, even though you may smell and taste the food, you'll have little secretory response from your stomach. That is why good appetites usually mean good digestion. Gastric juice which is secreted during this phase has a higher acidity and contains large amounts of pepsin. It is therefore a very active digestive secretion.

The presence of food in the stomach tends to neutralize and dilute the gastric hydrochloric acid. Thus, after your

82

meal, your stomach contents are never so acidic as is the gastric juice at the time of its initial formation. But if, for any reason, the secretion continues after your stomach is emptied, the acidity of the gastric contents rises to abnormally high levels, and under these circumstances it is possible for the gastric juice to damage the gastric or duodenal mucosa. One theory of the peptic ulcer formation is that gastric and duodenal ulcers are the result of continued secretion of gastric juice after the stomach has emptied itself and the neutralizing effect of the food is no longer present.

However, as Dr. Ellis pointed out, antacids stimulate the continued production of a great deal of acid even after the stomach has emptied, and to this extent antacids set the stage for ulcers.

What is the remedy for gastric distress? A little bit of hydrochloric acid.

On a trip to Italy recently, our family made sure we took along a bottle of HCL. We enjoyed the fabulous pasta dishes, the risottos, and the delicious pastries, many dishes we had never eaten before. We consumed quantities that exceeded an elegant sufficiency. We topped each big meal off with two HCL tablets and never knew a moment's distress. We offered HCL to our traveling companions who were feeling the discomfort of too much food and they were amazed at how quickly they felt relief from that overstuffed feeling.

Traveling, even though you are enjoying every moment of it, can be stressful and situations of stress tend to deplete your supply of hydrochloric acid.

Here's what happens when you don't have enough hydrochloric acid in your stomach. The emptying time of your stomach is slowed down. The pyloric valve will not open unless there is enough acid to trip the mechanism. You may go to bed feeling okay, but will wake up later with a burning in your stomach right behind the breastbone. You may get up and take some type of antacid, which will neutralize what little acid is in your stomach. This will make you feel better temporarily because you will get an overstimulation of the cells which produce HCL.

How does this happen? Dr. Dorn explained the process to me. The stomach just cannot stand to be alkaline. So when that bicarb hits it, it will go into a dither and start producing acid copiously. This triggers a dumping syndrome. The pyloric valve gets the acid message and opens prematurely. The masticated food, leaves your stomach all in a lump and you feel a sense of relief—for a little while. But wait. You must pay the piper. That food has not been properly acidified for your intestines to work on it. So in an hour or two, your intestines may begin to signal their distress with an attack of indigestion worse than the first. What happens is you are asking your intestines to carry out the digestion that should have been done in your stomach. Your intestines lack the enzymes necessary to carry out this phase of digestion.

More Than Stomach Comfort Is Involved

We can see, then, that "indigestion" signals a condition—insufficient hydrochloric acid—that can have more serious consequences than temporary distress.

Even if you are eating a perfectly good diet, if you lack the acid with which to utilize your proteins and minerals, you are going to suffer a deficiency of some sort which could lead to many problems—anemia, emaciation, arthritis, halitosis, allergies, itching of the rectum and other chronic diseases. If you lack hydrochloric acid, it is like having all the paraphernalia with which to build a good fire in your fireplace—but no match. That perfectly good diet is not going to do you much good unless you have the acid in your stomach to start the digestive process so that you can utilize your protein, your vitamins and your minerals to bring you the glow of health.

"You could eat a side of beef and be protein deficient," Dr. Ellis points out, "if you don't have the gastric acid to break it down." You can better assess the importance of hydrochloric acid when you consider that the protein you're not fully utilizing is absolutely vital to every cell, organ and tissue in your body—from the hair on your head to the nails on your toes and including your heart, kidneys, pancreas, thyroid gland, enzymes and hormones—they are all protein. Any one of these systems, or all of them, can suffer when you lack hydrochloric acid and therefore become protein deficient.

Without properly metabolized proteins you will be

deficient in all of the enzymes which control your muscles, the flow of your blood, and even the workings of your mind. You will also be deficient in antibodies which defend you against infection.

HCL can help protect you from disease by another route. "The acid secreted by the cells acts as an antiseptic or germicide and prevents putrefaction in the stomach," Dr. Jarvis points out. "When the acid is diminished or absent, there is no check on the growth of microorganisms in the stomach."

This facet of the many roles of hydrochloric acid was dramatically demonstrated when Dr. Hugh Tuckey of San Francisco, a pioneer in the use of HCL, found many of his patients who went to Mexico coming back with what is commonly called *turista*, a violent type of diarrhea accompanied by great pain. Antibiotics are frequently used as a means to counteract this *turista,* but Dr. Tuckey has seen people come back with the *turista* bacteria three or four years after their first attack.

When he gave each of his patients a bottle of hydrochloric acid tablets to take with them to Mexico, they never contracted *turista.* Tuckey and his wife always took hydrochloric acid with them when they went to Mexico and were able to enjoy their vacations without any of the devastation brought on by a bout with the runs.

Professor A. E. Austin tells in the book *Three Years of HCL Therapy* (out of print) these results of a deficiency or

86

absence of HCL: stagnation of pancreas, causing diabetes; stagnation of gall bladder, causing gallstones; putrefaction of the tissues, causing such conditions as pyorrhea, dyspepsia, nephritis (kidney disease), appendicitis, boils, abcesses, and pneumonia.

Dr. Walter B. Guy, one of the editors of the same volume, says that "deficiency of this hydrochloric peptic solution must, of necessity, bring about a slow starvation of the mineral elements, also a fixation of deposits in various tissues."

"Achlorhydria (no hydrochloric acid) is a common finding in cases of anemia. In fact," says Dr. Tuckey, "today no doctor will make a diagnosis of pernicious anemia without first establishing the diagnosis of a deficiency of HCL in the stomach." (*National Health Federation Bulletin*, January, 1967.)

Because anemia is so widespread in this country, some agencies are pushing for more iron fortification of common foods. But iron cannot be utilized without this essential acid. Neither can vitamin C, B vitamins or calcium. "In all the years of my practice," says Dr. Tuckey, "I never saw an arthritic patient, and I have treated them by the hundreds, who didn't have a deficiency of hydrochloric acid as well as a deficiency of calcium."

When hydrochloric acid is taken in liquid form, it should be taken through a straw and the mouth rinsed immediately lest it cause harm to the tooth enamel. Because of this danger, most doctors recommend tablets of glutamic acid hydrochloride or of hydrochloric betaine with pepsin.

Have You Enough?

How can you tell if you have a shortage of HCL? That's a good question. The medical test isn't any fun. It involves swallowing a tube and having the contents of your stomach pumped out for analysis. There are other ways that are less unpleasant.

Dr. Tuckey says that the patient usually reveals his own lack of HCL when he says "I can't drink fruit juice; it sours my stomach." This is a sure indication of a deficiency of HCL.

"Another symptom," says Dr. Tuckey, "is gas and bloating about an hour or two after eating. Halitosis is another."

Another symptom of low HCL or achlorhydria is burning in the stomach. This is a symptom which leads people to the antacid tablet. But the burning is usually caused by a lack of acid—not by hyperacidity. If hydrochloric acid tablets are used, the burning quickly disappears, says Dr. Tuckey.

Dr. Tuckey generally gives his patients one hydrochloric acid betaine with pepsin tablet at breakfast and lunch and two with dinner.

If by chance you should get too much HCL in your stomach after ingesting the tablets, within an hour or so you will have a burning in the stomach in which case you should take two or three glasses of water and subsequently cut your dosage in half.

Dr. Alan H. Nittler suggests this simple test to determine if your heartburn is caused by too little or too much acid. "Drink a solution of apple cider or wine vinegar (two teaspoons in one glassful of water) when you have heartburn. If you get almost immediate relief, your need is for more acid and not for antacids" (*A New Breed of Doctor*, Pyramid, 1972). If the vinegar intake aggravates the heartburn, then you are indeed producing too much acid. Try a glass or two of plain water. This dilutes the acid and frequently brings relief. You could, of course, take an antacid for quick relief but then you would face the risk of an acid rebound. Water alone will do the trick.

Must you continue taking HCL forever? At first, Dr. Tuckey found no other approach to normalizing the HCL in the stomach. But, after continual testing, he learned that by giving the patient a pancreatic tablet containing a duodenal substance together with the hydrochloric acid, he could generally normalize the HCL so that he could eventually take the patient completely off of it in from two to four months. In other words, he was providing the enzymes which promote the normal production of hydrochloric acid. One of the enzymes necessary to the production of this vital acid is pepsin.

Dr. Ellis suggests peppermint tea as a source of pepsin and, where there is a damaged mucous membrane, he suggests adding comfrey to the peppermint tea, thus providing a healing and soothing substance.

How widespread is the deficiency of HCL? Dr. Ellis

estimates that 90 percent of the people in this country are acid deficient. Bottle-fed babies run out of HCL by the time they reach their teens, he says. One of the enzymes necessary for the production of HCL is present in the very first secretions of the mother's breast. For this reason, Dr. Ellis insists that every newborn babe should be put to the breast immediately after birth, right there in the delivery room.

"In the 28 years of my practice," Dr. Ellis said, "I have never seen a patient with too much acid. On the contrary, practically everyone I've seen over 40 has a deficiency of HCL and practically everyone over 50 is achlorhydric (no HCL production at all).

What causes the shut-off of this essential acid? "The over use of alkalizers, for one thing," says Dr. Ellis. "Every time you take an alkalizer you whip your cells into a frenzy to get them to produce. By the time you're 50, your cells are completely worn out and are unable to produce any more HCL."

"Because of its particular prevalence in elderly people," says Dr. Norman Jolliffe, "achlorhydria should always be suspected in unexplained malnutrition and, conversely, malnutrition should be looked for in every patient having achlorhydria." (*Clinical Nutrition*, Harper Bros., 1962).

The nation's water supplies are further compounding our acid deficiency state, says Dr. Ellis. Because of all the chlorine and other bacteriocides that are poured into our polluted water, the PH of most water supplies is alkaline.

If you can't get pure mineral-rich water, use distilled water and take a good mineral supplement, Dr. Ellis suggests. That's what we do.

Sugar tends to neutralize the acid in the stomach and thus delays gastric emptying and starts the whole alkalizer merry-go-round. Since, as a nation, we are each consuming over 110 pounds of sugar every year, the sweet stuff is certainly compounding our digestive difficulties.

You might think, well, I never have heartburn or gastritis or such discomforts so I must have plenty of acid in my stomach. That's not always true. Dr. Royal Lee points out in the *Manual of Tropho-Therapy* (out of print) that "Many individuals are deficient in hydrochloric acid but evidence of gastro-intestinal symptoms is lacking. In these cases, pallor, fatigue, emaciation and other nonspecific indications may be due to deficiencies of protein, calcium, and iron, since these are best utilized in an acid medium, impaired in hydrochloric acid deficiency."

So, if your get-up-and-go has got up and gone, you, too, may lack HCL.

To build up your body's ability to produce HCL it would certainly be wise to eliminate sugar, drink only pure water, eat raw foods rich in enzymes and avoid chemicals in your foods, many of which are known to cripple your enzymes. At our house, we eat lots of sprouts—they're loaded with enzymes.

And do yourself a favor! Don't take alkalizers!

Pantothenic Acid Bursts the Bubble

"Your dinner was absolutely marvelous," Judge S. M. L. told our hostess at a recent dinner party. "The salad had just the right piquancy, the Beef Wellington was crusty and superb, everything was to the king's taste. But, maybe you have in your elegant kitchen a glass of plain soda water. I suffer with a condition which I can't politely discuss at the table."

"Me, too!" said Dr. K. P. another dinner guest.

"While you're getting it, I'll have some, too," laughed another guest.

You have no doubt guessed what condition the dinner guests were seeking to relieve. It's a condition which lacks emergency drama so you are not likely to see Dr. Welby agonize over it. Yet, our doctor guest told us, "It is more common than the common headache—especially in older people and it is, in fact, one of the most frequent and perplexing gastrointestinal complaints confronting the physician."

You might, however, get a more sympathetic reaction to the discomfort you feel around your middle if you call it "burbulence," a term coined by Ogden Nash and used by Dr. Avery Jones as a generic term to describe the various windy syndromes (*Practitioner* 198:367, 1967).

Times and manners have changed and with some of the changes have come more "burbulence." Today, though, belching or other embarrassing manifestions of "gas" is frowned on, so more and more of us experience the problem

92

and the recurring tug-of-war between disgrace and discomfort. A bubble of air trapped in the stomach or in a loop of bowel can cause great distress. It causes distention of the viscera, thus stretching the nerve endings in the intestinal wall and causing pain, bloating, and strange gurgling sounds.

Intestinal gas has two main sources, Dr. W. Grant Thompson points out in the *Canadian Medical Journal* (June 10, 1972). They are: air that is swallowed, and gases that are produced on location—usually in the colon. Carbonated beverages are an obvious source of gastrointestinal gas, as witness the gusty belching which is frequent background music in any beer parlor. Those who eat rapidly and gulp their meals may trap air along with their food. Gum chewing, thumb sucking, poorly fitting dentures and so on, cause excessive saliva production which must be swallowed —along with extra air.

If swallowed air does successfully pass the stomach, it may collect further down at the splenic or hepatic flexures of the colon. The result is abdominal distress. It is the inability to remove normal or increased amounts of air which leads to the symptoms of "burbulence," says Dr. Thompson.

Posture may also be important to the entrapment of air in the intestines, Dr. Thompson observes. To obtain relief, it's a good idea to take a stroll after meals or to get into the knee-chest position. Lie on a flat surface. A bed is fine. Bring both knees up to your chest for a count of ten. Then try the knee-chest position while lying on your stomach. Doctors sometimes recommend heat, massage, or a gentle enema to relieve the condition. All of these methods have variable results. Sometimes they help. Sometimes they don't.

Whatever its cause, doctors agree that excessive gas is a problem of no small proportions, one that sometimes sounds the ambulance siren in the dark of night because the pain it causes may be mistaken for heart pain. Dr. Manuel J. Rowen, a cardiologist associated with St. Elizabeth's Hospital in Elizabeth, New Jersey, says that "Gas causes pseudo angina. These... patients accumulate air in the gut. The pain it causes is referred to the precordium (the region over the heart or stomach). This they interpret as 'heart pain'" (*Western Medicine*, April, 1967).

Now, here's the good news. It has been found that pantothenic acid, a member of the vitamin B family which comes to your aid in times of stress, also comes to your aid to relieve intestinal gas and distention for which there is no physical cause. While air swallowing, as well as beans, cabbage, turnips, and carbonated beverages influence the gas we generate within ourselves, Dr. Rowen, Dr. Arnold Gelb and Dr. Jerome Weiss noted in *Western Medicine* that other factors influencing gaseousness are faulty digestion and gut motility. That's where the pantothenic acid comes in.

When dogs were fed a diet deficient in pantothenic acid, they had a loss of intestinal motility and as a consequence suffered the discomfort of abdominal

94

distention (Vitamin Information Bureau, Inc., N.Y.). Experiments also revealed that when pantothenic acid was given after surgery, there was a much shorter period of discomfort due to obstruction of the intestines which usually results from an inhibition of bowel motility, a condition known medically as ileus.

If you've ever had abdominal surgery, you know how wretchedly painful ileus can be. In its mildest and perhaps most common form, ileus causes post-operative distention with accompanying wind pains and abdominal discomfort. This may follow the simplest operation, possibly not even involving the abdomen, says an editorial in *The British Medical Journal* (September 14, 1963). In its severe form, fortunately rare, the intestines become completely paralyzed, all function ceases and the patient's life is in grave danger.

The finding that pantothenic acid lessened the period of ileus in dogs encouraged surgeons to evaluate the possibility of similar treatment in post-operative human patients.

Several investigators observed 100 patients suffering paralytic ileus and found that pantothenic acid produced good results with an early passage of flatus (gas, wind or air in the gastrointestinal tract) — (*American Journal of Surgery* (97:75; 1959). There was also much less postoperative nausea and distention.

When a double blind study of hospital patients was conducted, Drs. Nardi and Zuidema found a significant difference between the controls and the trial group. Those who got pantothenic acid were able to expel trapped gas in an average of ten hours. (*Surgery, Gynecology & Obstetrics,* 112:526; 1961). Compare their happiness at relief from abdominal distress with those who did not get pantothenic acid and suffered gas pains for 77 hours. Another boon to patient, hospital and hospitalization insurance or the patient's bankroll was the fact that length of stay in the hospital was considerably shorter for those who got the pantothenic (two days against 14 days). No adverse effects were observed.

How Pantothenic Acid Works

By what mechanism does pantothenic acid work to achieve this blessed relief from the distress which usually accompanies surgery? It seems that without pantothenic acid, a very important substance called acetylcholine cannot be produced. Acetylcholine is a chemical which transmits messages at the nerve endings. Without it, the nerves cannot do their thing—control motor and secretory intestinal activity. It has in fact been found in experimental animals, that after a period of stress, the acetylcholine reservoir in the body is diminished (*British Medical Journal,* September 14, 1963). However, if pantothenic acid is given, the acetylcholine level may be increased by as much as 50 percent. This was determined by Lynch, Spurgeon and Worton (*Journal of Applied Nutrition,* 11:117, 1958). Another team of researchers, Polacek, Close and Ellison reported in *Surgical Forum* (11:325, 1960) that in experiments on dogs, the administration of pantothenic acid during the postoperative period shortened the duration of the ileus.

These experiments suggest that the stress of abdominal operations produces a depletion of the supply of acetylcholine, which in turn causes a varying degree of intestinal atony or loss of motility in the intestinal muscle, and that the administration of pantothenic acid, by preventing such depletion, also prevents the development of ileus.

But what about the person who hasn't been anywhere near the operating room and still suffers all the distress of "burbulence"? What can pantothenic acid do for him? Since pantothenic acid is a component of the co-enzymes concerned in the formation of acetylcholine, unless we get enough pantothenic acid to prevent the depletion of acetylcholine, we're going to lose gut motility, a condition which is related to the ileus suffered by post-operative patients, a condition which sets the stage for "burbulence."

How much pantothenic acid do you need? This depends on you and your chemistry. Dr. Roger Williams suggests in *Nutrition Against Disease* (Pitman, 1971) that "some may have much higher needs than others." The Food and Nutrition Board of the National Academy of Sciences— National Research Council recommends a daily intake of 10 milligrams. But your requirements, especially if you're suffering with "burbulence," may be considerably higher. An increased need for pantothenic acid seems to run in families and some families have been shown to require as much as 20 times more of this vitamin in order to maintain health than others, Dr. Williams points out.

Carlton Fredericks, PhD., reported in his *Newsletter of Nutrition* (October 1, 1972) that "250 milligrams daily has not only been reported to relieve postoperative gas pains, but to prevent them. My recent observations," he says, "suggest that those who are troubled by intestinal gas and distention for which no physical cause has been found sometimes respond to pantothenic acid—so much so that I am persuaded that these people have an elevated requirement for the vitamin, difficult to fulfill even with a reasonable choice of foods."

Where do you find pantothenic acid?

It was once thought that because pantothenic acid is distributed so widely, the chances of developing a serious deficiency were slight. But since the growth of food processing and other vitamin-damaging influences on the food supply, available vitamins in our foods decrease every year. Pantothenic acid is present in the germ of all grains. It is therefore sacrificed when flour is refined and not restored in the enrichment farce. We should, therefore, make certain to use those foods which are particularly rich in pantothenic acid in order to prevent even a marginal deficiency. Nutritional yeast, liver, wheat germ, kidney, heart, salmon, and eggs are among our best sources of pantothenic acid.

If the windy syndrome is causing you discomfort and embarrassment, try getting more exercise and more pantothenic acid (also known as calcium pantothenate) and chances are you will no longer feel like Ogden Nash when he wrote, "I feel as unfit as an untuned fiddle, and it is the result of a certain turbulence of the mind and a certain 'burbulence' in the middle."

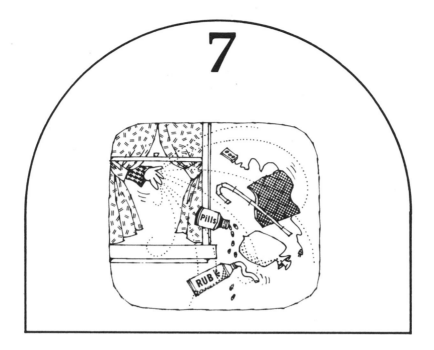

Grow Old without Arthritis

I never realized what a heartbreaker arthritis could be until I worked at the local hospital and witnessed the daily stream of people—young as well as old—hobbling in on canes or crutches or being pushed in wheelchairs to the rehabilitation department. There they were massaged, whirlpooled, ultra-sounded, treated with hot wax, put through a range of motion exercises, then given a stiff bill, an encouraging smile and told to come in three times a week.

Many of the older arthritis patients were puffy from cortisone. They were subject to fractures, and many were confined to wheelchairs. Their charts revealed their doctors prescriptions for aspirin, pain killers, cortisone derivatives— never, and I mean never, did I see a doctor's order for vitamins or minerals. And it's a shame because there is much evidence that when diet is corrected and the proper vitamins added, arthritis is curable and preventable.

If you are one of the many millions afflicted with the pain and desperation of arthritis, do yourself a favor and try the nutritional approach. A distinguished orthopedic physician in California has been proving for the past 25 years that it works.

Robert Bingham, M.D., well-known and highly-respected California physician, has been bringing health, help, and a new lease on life to hundreds of patients. He does this without the use of dangerous drugs. "No person who is in good nutritional health develops either rheumatoid or osteoarthritis," he says (*The Journal of Applied Nutrition,* Winter, 1972).

The patient with rheumatoid arthritis, Dr. Bingham points out, has a history of not getting enough of the right kinds of food, and is usually nervous, tense, anxious, overactive, has poor resistance to infection and has a history of chronic inflammatory infectious diseases.

The patient with osteoarthritis on the other hand has frequently had too much to eat, but of the worst kinds of foods—refined flour substances, too many sweets, and fats.

While in no instance did the doctors ever find a case of rheumatoid arthritis developing in a patient with a good dietary history, osteoarthritis is sometimes triggered by a recent illness, injury, or operation. (All these stress conditions deplete the body of nutrients, especially vitamin

C.) Barring such nutrient-depleting stresses, Dr. Bingham describes the typical patient with osteoarthritis as middle-aged or elderly; overweight; poorly nourished on a high carbohydrate diet; deficient in protein, vitamins and enzymes for a period of months to years before the onset of his arthritis.

In view of these findings, it is not surprising that, as people turn in increasing numbers to empty-calorie foods, the incidence of arthritic diseases climbs proportionately. A survey of chronic arthritis in the United States, reported in the 1967 *Journal of Arthritis and Rheumatism,* reveals that four to five million people in the United States have rheumatoid arthritis and 50 to 60 million people have osteoarthritis.

These figures roughly parallel those of the Department of Agriculture's 1968 survey to determine the extent of malnutrition in this country. As many as 50 percent of the households surveyed were below standard levels in calcium, vitamin A, vitamin C, milk, vegetables and fruits.

Finally, as a cause of arthritis, it has been pointed out that there is a "rheumatoid personality." Dr. Bingham grants that severe mental and emotional distress can lead to the crippling disease. But here again, he demonstrates, it comes down to nutritional disorder.

"Nutritionists know that nervous and mental and emotional stress interfere with appetite, digestion, absorption of food, the choices of food, nutritional habits and dietary patterns. Emotional stress exerts a control on the glands of internal secretion, particularly the thyroid, adrenals and pituitary, and they play an important role in bone and joint metabolism. Naturally, any disturbance in the nervous and emotional function of a person produces biological changes which can affect the bones or joints."

Dr. Bingham maintains that not only is arthritis preventable through good nutrition, but arthritis is also curable.

He speaks from experience. For the past 16 years in Desert Hot Springs, California, he and his associates have carried out a remarkably successful program of complete therapy which has emphasized the role of nutrition in the treatment of arthritic diseases.

The program which they have devised could serve as a blueprint for any doctor sincerely interested in helping his arthritic patients without using dangerous drugs.

First, they make a list of each patient's likes and dislikes, those foods which agree or disagree and those foods to which the patient claims to have allergies. At the same time the orthopedic examination records the patient's height, weight, and posture. Nutritional status is recorded along with comments regarding signs of deficiency in the hair, skin, eyes, teeth, fingernails, and toenails, fat distribution and muscular development.

Each patient is given a printed diet list which recommends foods which are beneficial for bone growth, development, repair and the prevention of disease and

physical deterioration. This guide also includes a list of no-no's.

Lose Weight and Improve Nutrition

For the patient with osteoarthritis, the commonest dietary modification required is increasing the protein and calcium intake and adding supplemental vitamins, trace minerals and anabolic hormones.

Since these patients are usually overweight, Dr. Bingham suggests increased protein in the form of fortified low fat milk or dairy products which also provide well-absorbed calcium. Other forms of calcium which he suggests are six oyster-shell tablets a day or six bone meal tablets a day. Vitamin D is very important for osteoarthritic patients. Dr. Bingham recommends 1,000 I.U. from natural sources like halibut liver oil together with 25,000 units daily of vitamin A. This is for the treatment phase. For prevention he suggests half of this amount.

A radical change in dietary habits is usually necessary to bring about improvement in the rheumatoid arthritic patients. Here is a typical program as suggested by Dr. Bingham:

1. Confine the patient to bedrest, 16 hours a day.

2. Increase the patient's water consumption to eight glasses a day.

3. Gradually decrease all drugs to the minimum the patient can take without too much pain. Reduce and slowly eliminate all corticosteroid medications.

4. Place the patient on a high protein diet.

5. Serve the patient fresh, raw, natural foods whenever possible using a grinder or blender if necessary.

6. Eliminate tobacco, alcohol, refined carbohydrates and saturated fats.

7. Prescribe vitamins, minerals, hormones, and enzymes.

Since patients with rheumatoid arthritis are usually deficient in protein and in vitamin C, Dr. Bingham recommends 2,000 mg. of natural vitamin C each day and three glasses a day of raw milk which supplies both protein and calcium. Certified milk is preferable he says, because it contains an anti-stiffness factor which is destroyed by pasteurization. Where raw milk is not available, pasteurized is acceptable.

Dr. Bingham emphasizes that "It is important to keep in mind that to preserve natural food intact (including proteins and amino acids which have not been damaged by heat; hormones and enzymes which have not been altered by cooking, drying, storage or preservation; and vitamins in the highest biological efficiency), the food must be as fresh and ripe as possible; grown by organic methods; free of residues of poisonous pesticides and fertilizers; and delivered and prepared in as natural and palatable a form as possible."

While most doctors discourage initiative on the part of their patients, Dr. Bingham has found that the most improvement resulted when intelligent and well-motivated patients cooperated by studying and learning as much about good nutrition as they could in order to help in the

management of their own arthritic problems. In fact, the only failures have occurred in patients who would not learn or could not accept a new dietary plan, or who would not give up certain habits such as alcohol, tobacco, and the over-use of pain relieving, tranquilizing and hypnotic drugs.

In spite of the fact that your doctor has probably told you that diet has nothing to do with your arthritis, one of Dr. Bingham's patients was moved to say, "Good nutrition is the only thing that has helped me." Another commented, "I started getting better when I changed my diet." And another said "Why didn't my other doctors tell me these things about food and nutrition?"

I do not recommend that you attempt to treat yourself for either form of arthritis. Treatment is far more complicated and varied than could be indicated in the scope of this book, and really must be professionally supervised.

What I do recommend is that the arthritic find a doctor who practices nutritionally. That's his best hope of avoiding permanent crippling and pain.

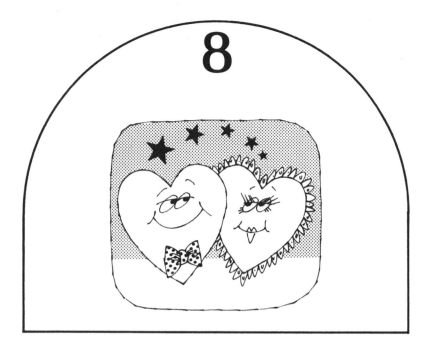

Help Yourself to a Healthy Heart

Many people, as they grow older, feel that they must limit their eggs, butter, cream, and cheesecake, lest the cholesterol do them in. They use margarine and tasteless substitutes for all the good things in life and feel virtuous about it. Many of them are being done in by their own "virtue."

I do believe that this was the case with Laurie J., an old schoolmate of mine. This girl had such beauty and brains that she was voted not only the prettiest girl in the class, but the most likely to succeed. Succeed she did—in many areas. She got her MRS. before she got her BA. When she married Doug, he was doing a residency in internal medicine.

Though we kept in touch by phone and mail, 30 years

had elapsed since high school graduation before I saw Laurie again. Doug had been one of the year's victims of sudden death due to coronary thrombosis and Laurie was coming to visit some of her old friends in our part of the country.

I was excited about her impending visit and communicated this excitement to our kids, whose help I needed to get the house in order. I described Laurie to them as I remembered her—pretty as a movie star, with flaming red hair, a quick smile and a figure that always elicited long, low whistles.

When Laurie finally arrived for her visit, my first sight of her was something of a shock. Why, she's an old lady, I thought and wondered if she was thinking the same thing about me, if perhaps the years did things to you when you weren't looking.

Laurie, I found out over the weekend, had not exactly neglected herself—on the contrary. She did everything that the doctor ordered—zealously. Laurie was a good sport though. It's a good thing. A breakfast that could have been a disaster turned out to be a circus. My husband scrambled the eggs. (Scrambled eggs is his specialty—nobody can make them as light and fluffy as he can. I think he talks to them like he talks to the African violets.) He brought the eggs to the table triumphantly and ladled out a serving on Laurie's plate.She inhaled the fragrance appreciatively. "I love eggs," she said—"two a week, that's all I'm allowed. Cholesterol you know. I assume they're made with margarine."

"Margarine!" I exclaimed. "We don't use margarine. It's hydrogenated!"

After breakfast, when we were taking our vitamin supplements, Laurie popped her hormone pill (for eternal youth) and another pill (to prevent an angina attack from all that cholesterol) into her mouth.

I have gone to considerable lengths to tell you about Laurie because I think that she is typical. So many people today live in fear of a heart attack. They pass up all the pleasures of the dining room table and stick to diets devoid of butter and eggs. They don't dare take a turn around the dance floor. The irony of it is that in spite of their adherence to the life of self-denial, or maybe because of it, The Grim Reaper cuts them down way ahead of their time.

I'd like to tell you about the experience of Dr. Jacobus Rinse. Because he suffered a coronary attack, Dr. Rinse did some thorough investigating and came up with a different kind of diet. Now, at 73, he is hale and hearty and enjoying life immensely. He is busily hewing wood for some outbuildings on his farm.

Dr. Rinse, who has a PhD. in chemistry, suffered an attack of angina due to atherosclerosis back in 1951 and was warned at that time by his doctor that he had ten years to live, "if you avoid all physical activity."

Did Dr. Rinse accept that verdict and stagnate? He did not. He applied to his own problem the same operating procedure which he used so successfully as a consulting chemist. He made a study of the literature, set up a working hypothesis and started to experiment.

The result is a breakfast dish which he says has taken the ache out of his ailing heart. But, it has done more than that. He says the same breakfast which he concocted as a cure for his atherosclerosis has kept him free of colds, flu, infections, arthritis, bursitis and backache.

To get back to step one of Dr. Rinse's plan—a study of the literature. The more he studied accepted medical doctrine, the more puzzled he became. According to that doctrine, the heart attack which felled him chose the wrong victim. Because, according to medical do's and don'ts, he was definitely not a candidate for a heart attack. He confessed to none of the habits which doctors warn will lead one down the path of narrowed arteries to atherosclerosis. He did not smoke; he was not overweight, he had no special tensions, no family history of the disease, and he got plenty of exercise.

There's something definitely wrong with medical doctrine, he reasoned. But, by the same token, he must have been doing something wrong! What?

Because he was a chemist, he likened the body to a chemical plant which produces various kinds of energy for moving, for thinking, for electrical energy and for heat. What does a chemical plant need? Fuel, of course. But that's not all it needs. It needs secondary materials to serve as catalysts, lubricants, and emulsifiers, to expedite processing of the primary materials. Does that sound like a chemistry

textbook? Well that's the way Dr. Rinse thinks, and that's the way he talks.

So, what are the secondary materials which the body needs? Minerals, vitamins, and enzymes, all necessary to the many chemical reactions of metabolism, to produce energy, and new tissue from proteins, fats and carbohydrates. Since the body needs all these primary raw materials, Dr. Rinse hypothesized, "Foods must contain everything in adequate quantities and should be varied as much as possible."

"Aha," he told himself, "there must be a missing nutritional link in my diet. What can it be? Perhaps it is enzymes." He began to experiment with enzyme-rich foods like raw herring, raw eggs, red meat, uncooked vegetables and yogurt. He was not able to determine whether any of these foods had an effect on his well-being. A funny thing happened though when he tried garlic—and you should make a note of this—he found that he was able to indulge in greater activity without the usual increase in pressure or pain in the breast.

Dr. Rinse did not stop there. Because he had good experience with vitamin C for curing and preventing colds and flu, he increased his intake to one gram (1,000 milligrams) every day. Vitamin C helps to convert cholesterol to bile acid. It is also an antioxident. Then he added a multi-vitamin-and-mineral tablet just to make sure that he was touching all the bases. He didn't stop there. He fortified his breakfast cereal with wheat germ and yeast. On the advice of the Doctors Shute of London, Ontario, he took

300 units of vitamin E after each meal. He avoided strenuous exercise and managed a more or less normal life with only occasional heart pain for several years.

Then, in 1957—whamo—another heart attack.

There's nothing like coming close to the Pearly Gates to make life look beautiful. Every daybreak is a work of art to be savored with all one's senses. Dr. Rinse wanted very much to increase the number of his days on earth. He set himself to renewing his avid search for more information and found a study in which rats and rabbits, who got lecithin or safflower oil, experienced a lowering of the cholesterol content of their blood. He decided to add a tablespoon of each to his breakfast "mash."

Miracle of miracles! In only a few days, his heart spasms stopped and his elevated pulse rate diminished slightly. After three months on this "breakfast," all symptoms of angina, even after exercising, had disappeared! One year later, his capacity for heavy outdoor work and running had returned!

Now, 16 years later, he has had no recurrence of his angina.

While this breakfast of nutrients worked for Dr. Rinse, would it work for others? To find out, he put his experiences in writing and gave copies to people who were interested. These are some of the results:

Dr. W. suffered a cerebral thrombosis and heart infarct at the age of 53. Six months after going on Rinse's mash, he was working full time and has had no relapse since. He is convinced that the breakfast has helped to cure him.

A 69-year old executive of Dutch Industries had a blood clot in one of his legs. He was, on doctor's orders, using anticoagulants and following a strict diet without eggs and butter. After learning about Dr. Rinse's experience, he followed the same regimen and cured himself rapidly.

A Dutch mechanical engineer, age 48, had such severe angina that he had to stop working and found no relief from drugs prescribed by heart specialists. After two months on the breakfast, he could run again and works now, at times in deep freeze storage rooms, without any bad effects.

A 72-year old consulting chemist from Texas who had suffered several heart attacks went on Rinse's breakfast and improved rapidly. He stopped his prescribed medicines and is now back at work.

A 70-year old woman of Manchester, Vermont, had suffered a blocked artery in the neck and partial paralysis. In December, 1967, she started with the food supplements. Her health improved rapidly and she has had no recurrences.

A Dutch internist reported that he had prescribed the breakfast to many older patients with spectacular results. Many of them resumed their activities even after having been invalids for a long time.

A chemist wrote that he was able to regulate his wife's blood pressure with what he called "Rinse's morning feed."

A man in Chicago wrote that he had cured himself of

arthritis and two friends of bursitis by using the food supplements.

Today there are several thousand people in Holland and the U.S.A. and some in England and Belgium who are using Rinse's morning feed. What do doctors think of it? Some physicians advise their patients not to use the supplements, while most simply ignore the method, and continue to prescribe anticoagulants to thin the blood and nitroglycerol tablets for the pain. Both these medications must be used with extreme caution because of side effects.

The ingredients in Dr. Rinse's breakfast can be taken with safety and with variations suited to one's case and need. Dr. Rinse feels that the most important components in his breakfast are lecithin and polyunsaturated oil.

Dr. Rinse's Mash Recipe

He makes a mixture of one tablespoon each of granulated soybean lecithin (rich in phosphorous), debittered yeast, and raw wheat germ, and one teaspoon of bone meal (rich in calcium). He makes this recipe up in large quantities and stores it in a dark place to protect the vitamins from damaging light rays. Then he mixes two tablespoons of this mixture in a bowl, with one tablespoon of dark brown or raw sugar and one tablespoon of safflower oil or other linoleate oil, such as soybean. He dissolves this mixture in milk, and adds yogurt to improve the consistency. He adds cold cereal for calories as needed, or else mixes it with hot cereal such as oatmeal or porridge. Raisins and other fruits may be added as desired.

For severe cases of atherosclerosis, he suggests doubling the quantity of lecithin to two tablespoons. He also recommends a daily intake of 500 milligrams of vitamin C, 100 I.U. of vitamin E, and one multi-vitamin-mineral tablet.

Eggs and butter may be included in this diet. But no hard margarine.

Many doctors would indeed be horrified at these suggestions. All that cholesterol? You're mad!

Doctors go into a dither about cholesterol because statistically the chances of developing atherosclerosis are greater if the cholesterol count of the blood is high. Yet, Dr. Rinse points out, many persons who have a high cholesterol count are healthy. Further, "It has been demonstrated that the liver produces more cholesterol if food contains less." It is doubtful, therefore, Dr. Rinse says, if efforts to lower cholesterol by avoidance of such food as eggs or butter or the use of drugs that affect the production of cholesterol in the liver are justified. "Reducing its production by means of drugs can be dangerous and has caused serious side effects, such as cataracts and the loss of hair," Dr. Rinse asserts.

Keeping Cholesterol in Solution

"If lecithin is added to the diet, the unwanted deposits of cholesterol derivatives do not form, because the lecithin-cholesterol compound is soluble," Dr. Rinse explains. It flows smoothly through the arteries and does not clot. Both cholesterol and lecithin occur in eggs and therefore, says Dr. Rinse, an atherosclerotic patient should not deprive himself of the pleasures and good wholesome nutrition found in eggs.

"Since the main problem of atherosclerosis is to keep cholesterol in solution, and since polyunsaturated lecithin has the propensity to dissolve cholesterol deposits in the arterial wall, then it is apparent that the diet should contain lecithin in sufficient amounts," Dr. Rinse maintains. "Lecithin occurs naturally in nuts, seeds, eggs and soybeans and is produced in commercial quantities from soybean oil."

As Roger J. Williams points out in his book *Nutrition Against Disease,* "It is known that lecithin has soap-like characteristics, is a powerful emulsifying agent and its presence in the blood tends to dissolve cholesterol deposits."

While many doctors are now recommending polyunsaturated oils to the exclusion of all saturates, Dr. Rinse points out that only in the presence of sufficient lecithin, can the polyunsaturated fatty acids help in dissolving cholesterol. "In countries with high fish consumption, such as Norway, the addition of polyunsaturated oils alone did not have any effect. It is lecithin that they need."

At the same time—and this is perhaps the very heart of Dr. Rinse's theory—lecithin cannot properly do its job except in the presence of adequate amounts of linoleate—the chief polyunsaturate.

When Does Cholesterol Melt?

Cholesterol is an aromatic alcohol with a melting point of 149 degrees centigrade. At body temperature cholesterol is a solid fat. When combined with lecithin the melting point becomes much lower. At what point does the cholesterol-lecithin complex change from the solid to the liquid state? The transition point varies with the degree of saturation of the fatty acids in the blood—70 degrees centigradc (about 160 degrees fahrenheit) with stearate and 0 degrees (32 degrees fahrenheit) with linoleate.

The incidence of atherosclerosis then can be related to the melting point of the cholesterol derivatives. Too little lecithin and too little linoleate and the deposits will be solid at body temperature and will boggle your bloodstream and form plaques. The lecithin must contain sufficient quantity of linoleate groups to cause the complex cholesterol to melt at or below blood temperature. That's why Dr. Rinse uses the unsaturated oil—to increase the proportion of linoleates. Lecithin in itself does not contain sufficient linoleate to lower the melting point of the cholesterol adequately, according to Dr. Rinse's calculations.

The daily requirement for lecithin and polyunsaturated fatty acids and cholesterol are the same—a few grams per day. The molecular weight of lecithin is twice that of cholesterol so one needs four to six grams of lecithin and an equal amount of linoleate every day.

If the atherosclerosis is advanced, the amounts of lecithin and oil should be increased. Sometimes it takes only a little more lecithin to tip the see-saw in favor of healthy arteries.

When Dr. F. S. P. Van Buchem and the Gaubius Institute in Leiden, Holland, analyzed the blood of 48 men between 40 and 60 years of age, half of whom had atherosclerotic complications, those men having a lecithin content of 36 percent or higher in their blood fats showed no atherosclerosis, whereas those with 34 percent or lower all had the disease (*Ned. Tydschr. v. Geneeskunde*, 115, 1311, 1971).

Dr. Rinse is now 73 years old, hale and hearty, and, he told me, he can match any man half his age for heavy work and endurance. His breakfast mash and vitamin program has gained several thousand adherents and, he said, several doctors are using it themselves and recommending it to patients.

We now have in our refrigerator a jar labeled "Dr. Rinse's Mash" and we enjoy some every day—on top of cereal, with yogurt, with milk, with sour cream and bananas. I add it to bread recipes, cookies and cakes and to crumb crusts for pies and cheesecake. I'd like to suggest it to all of those who are denying themselves the pleasures of good eating and are chalking up wrinkles and heart pains instead of points in the book of life.

I say, "Live it up!" Enjoy eggs, enjoy the real spread, enjoy life. But, count among your joys every day, a bowl of Dr. Rinse's magic concoction.

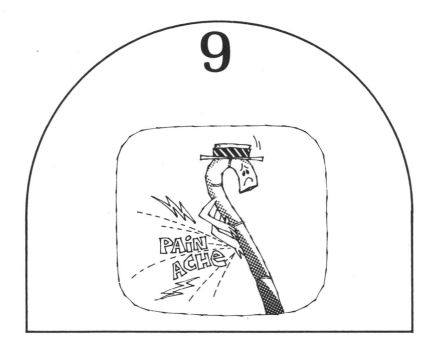

Happiness Is a Back
That Doesn't Ache!

Mr. J. M., who is well into his seventies, gave us his calling card last Saturday. It said "Retired—no business, no money, no ulcers—" "I'd be a happy man," he told us, "but my back won't let me."

For millions of older people, happiness is just having a back that doesn't ache. Almost every one of us who has achieved middle age has also experienced the excruciating pain of an aching back. Some two million Americans will be initiated into the "Bad Back Club" this year, bringing the total membership to a whopping 70 million, or one out of every three adults in this nation. In fact, according to the U.S. Public Health Service, there are at this very moment seven million of us hobbling painfully to medicine men to have our aching backs stretched, straightened, hot packed, cold packed, massaged, manipulated or gently patted.

It might hearten you to know that the chances of dying of a bad back are practically nil. It is also good to know that surgery is not often required to cure a bad back. Only about one out of twenty people with bad backs will ever need an operation, says Dr. Leon Root, a New York orthopedic surgeon and co-author, with Thomas Kiernan, of the book, *Oh My Aching Back* (David McKay, 1973).

I realize that these statistics bring you little comfort when you are doubled over with a backache.

However, there are steps you can take right now, which can help you live a happy life without a backache, or if you do have one, will help you handle it with common sense, so that your first episode does not lead to a lifetime of agony.

Dr. Root, who sees many aching backs in the course of a day, says that the great majority of the back ailments he treats could have been avoided through the application of a little practical knowledge and common sense when the first ache or spasm manifested itself.

According to the Health Insurance Institute (*Health Insurance News,* November, 1973), you should not try to diagnose the problem yourself. Your best course is to consult a doctor or orthopedist immediately. Chances are he will suggest getting into bed with a heating pad. Fine. When every move is a torment, that sounds like heaven. But what kind of a bed are you going to fall into? Is the mattress firm enough to support your back and yet not so firm that it

prevents your muscles from relaxing?

When we get down to the nitty gritty, a mattress is perhaps the most important article of furniture, if you can call it that, in the whole house. Perhaps we do not give enough attention to the coils that support our backs night after night. A better choice of mattress might have helped to prevent that aching back in the first place. Do not be fooled into thinking that the firmer the mattress the better it is for you. This is not necessarily so. Judith Hann, who surveyed the ups and downs of bedding for bad backs in Great Britain (*New Scientist,* May 3, 1973) reports that a bed which is too hard can prevent relaxation because the body will not be cradled, thus leaving unsupported hollows so that muscles cannot relax.

A small firm in England has just produced a completely new type of mattress which combines differential areas of softness and hardness so that the spine can remain straight. Where the body protrudes—at the shoulder and hip—the mattress is much softer, with firm sections for the head, legs and the spinal area. We could find no counterpart of this particular mattress available in the U.S. But there are several lines which offer mattresses which are firm and yet conform to the body's contours (Beautyrest, Serta, Perfect Sleeper, Sealy Posturepedic, Stearns and Foster, etc.). These are available at various furniture and department stores.

In England, as in the United States, the sale of firmer mattresses has been booming. Several manufacturers have carried out research projects to find out why people are changing to extra firm beds. One effort involved putting three beds in a hall to discover what 500 testers thought of the medium, firm, and orthopedic mattresses. The orthopedic model was the firmest mattress in the range used on top of a bedboard. Over one-third of the testers preferred this rigid bed, although only half of them suffered from bad backs, reports Miss Hann.

But there is often a difference between what you judge to be comfortable in a quick test, and what you later find gives you the best night's rest. A local furniture store told me that they sold 24 extra-firm mattresses last year, but took back 12.

Your weight has a great deal to do with the firmness of the mattress you should choose. The heavier you are, the firmer the mattress should be. Even foam rubber comes in various degrees of firmness and you can find the right type. Plastic foam tends to soften with use and I don't recommend it.

Now that you have your good mattress, what else can you do to get the kink out of your back?

Pain Relieved by Crawling

One woman discovered quite by chance that a baby's method of locomotion worked wonders for her. Mrs.Luther Avirett of Dunedin, Florida told *Life Magazine* editors (April 30, 1965) that she was bending over when she suddenly felt as though she'd been punched hard in the back.

She had been pacing the floor for nearly six hours in a bent-over position when her husband summoned her to witness the birth of a baby fish. Since she was unable to stand, stoop or sit, she dropped to her hands and knees to peer into the tank. The relief from pain, she said, was almost instant. She felt so good she crawled like a baby for nearly 15 minutes. When she tried to upright herself, she found she could stand—almost straight. She crawled several times a day for a week and all soreness in her back vanished.

Some people find that a good stretch will help reposition whatever it is that has gone out of whack. One woman told me that she had suffered with a bad back all her life. All she had to do was sneeze and one of her vertebrae would pop out of place and she would have to go through many weeks of back adjustments. It got so bad that she had x-rays and sought the help of specialists who told her she needed a back operation. This she refused.

Then she got this advice, from another sufferer, which relieved her misery.

"Put up a one-inch pipe (not any larger or it will hurt your hands when you are hanging from it) on your back porch or wherever it is convenient for you," she was told. "Put it up high enough so that when you stretch from the bar your feet do not touch the floor."

At first you will not be able to hang there for any length of time because it really hurts, but gradually you can work up to almost a minute. Do this two or three times a day. It works something like traction. In fact, you can really hear all your bones snap, crackle and pop.

If you don't happen to have a chinning bar handy when you first feel that awful "spoing" in your back, you might try suspending yourself from the top of a door frame holding on with both hands. That's what my husband did at a party after he bent over to put down an empty glass and froze in that position. First he sagged slowly and carefully to the floor, and when he was able to get to his feet with some help from bystanders, he did the door-suspension act.

At home we have a chinning bar in the pantry doorway. Using it usually helps. If it doesn't, we visit a nearby chiropractor for an adjustment.

Vitamin C Plays a Big Role

Vitamin C is one of the nutrients which can prevent or come to the aid of an aching back. So says Dr. James Greenwood, Jr., of Baylor University College of Medicine, Houston, Texas, who told me that he insists on more vitamin C for all patients with back problems. "We have seen that large doses of vitamin C help patients with back, neck or leg pain due to spinal disc injuries. Some people have been able to avoid the necessity for surgery and others have been able to avoid returns of the syndrome when their vitamin C intake was greatly increased."

The relationship between vitamin C and the building of bones, blood vessels, cartilage and collagen has, in fact, been long established. One of the most definite physiological functions of vitamin C is that of assisting in the formation of collagen for the maintenance of stability and

126

elasticity of connective tissues generally. And this would include the bones, cartilage, muscles and vascular tissues.

It was this relationship of vitamin C to the building of collagen which first prompted Dr. Greenwood to try vitamin C for his own personal stab in the back which had been keeping him on and off the heating pad for a period of ten years while his pain grew more excruciating with each attack.

About four months after he started taking 100 mgs. of vitamin C three times a day, he noticed that he was comfortable and able to exercise without difficulty. Serving as his own control, Dr. Greenwood cut the vitamin C out of his daily schedule. He was promptly back on the heating pad. When he resumed taking vitamin C, his back improved.

Then the Texas neurosurgeon applied the benefits of his own experience to more than 500 patients with back pain. They reported gratifying relief even when the pain was caused by a slipped disc.

Dr. Greenwood recommends 250 mgs. three times a day with an increase to 1,000 or 1,500 mgs. daily if there is any discomfort, or if heavy exercise is anticipated. Some patients he said, need 1,500 to 2,000 mgs. a day.

Further evidence of the value of vitamin C as a preventive of muscle stiffness comes from D. I. H. Syed, a London physician who wrote in the correspondence columns of the *British Medical Journal* (July 30, 1966), that "Muscle stiffness which arises after exercise or unaccustomed work can be prevented or treated by taking massive doses of ascorbic acid."

Dr. Syed found that 500 mg. of vitamin C before exercise and 400 mg. after exercise, together with plenty of fluids, were usually sufficient to prevent stiffness developing next morning. "But if it does develop, it is usually very slight and is easily cleared up by taking 400 additional mg. of vitamin C and extra fluids, and if required one or two hourly doses of 200 mg."

As Dr. Syed explained, "Vitamin C looks after the endothelial lining of the capillaries. Therefore it may prevent damage or puncture of these capillaries in muscles during exercise. It may also help detoxification of metabolites and by its diuretic effect help with excretion."

Another factor which could be responsible for the pain in your back is fluorides, chemicals that get into our environments in great quantities. Backaches are high on the list of troubles that were forecast as the inevitable result of our introduction of artificial fluorides into the environment.

F. B. Exner, M.D. and C. L. Waldbott, M.D., tell us of back troubles caused by fluorides in the *American Fluoridation Experiment* (Devin Adair, 1961). Rheumatoid spondylitis, a back disability that strikes men between the ages of 20 and 40; poker back (pain and stiffness in the back area), and limitation of motion in the spine are some of the back problems associated with fluorosis. One woman whose main complaint was backache was diagnosed as suffering from fluorine intoxication from drinking water.

If your doctor has determined that your problem is

HAPPINESS IS A BACK THAT DOESN'T ACHE

muscular, you should avoid the rigid posture that many backachers assume, say Ellen B. Lagerfwerff and Karen A. Perlroth, authors of the book, *Mensendieck Your Posture and Your Pains* (Doubleday, 1973).

Generally the reaction to a sensation of discomfort is to hold the body rigid, the authors point out. But a rigid body cultivates muscular pains. "As a rule, if you sense discomfort in your muscles, move. Usually, this will bring about the longed-for relief immediately." At first it may be agony to break through the barrier of pain. But movement in and around the affected area will eventually release the muscular pain. Any on-and-off muscular activity is better than no movement at all, say the authors of this excellent do-it-yourself posture correction book, who studied the Mensendieck System in Holland and are in private practice in California.

There's a difference between relieving symptoms and taking care of the problem. Good nutrition, lots of vitamin C and the correct alignment of your body, whether you are sitting, standing, walking or resting, can do more than you realize to get at the basic causes of the ache in your back that makes you so happy when it goes away.

If You Must Go
To the Hospital

I hope that your only contact with hospitals is for visiting purposes. When you do go, do the patient a favor: do not bring cut flowers. Water in which they rest has been found to harbor harmful bacteria which your friend may not have the strength to fight, especially when he's down and out.

What should you bring your hospitalized friend? You should of course let the gift fit the patient's condition. If there are no diet restrictions, I usually bring a lovely dish filled with what I call "survival snacks"—a mixture of pumpkin seeds, sunflower seeds, sesame seeds, raw cashews and unsulphured raisins, sprinkled with unsweetened coconut crumbs. They love it and, I found out, so do the nurses and the guests. Now I take two bowls—"one for guests and one for you."

Homemade chicken soup with brown rice is another of my frequent offerings. I once met my friend, the rabbi, in the elevator of the hospital. He was carrying a jar of chicken soup. "How very nice of you to consider your patient's body as well as his soul," I remarked, pointing to the bottle under his arm.

"This," he said holding up the jar, "is true religion. All the rest is ritual."

Since fresh fruit is very scarce on the hospital menu, it is a most welcome gift. I do not send a prepared steamer basket, which is frequently kept around uneaten because it looks pretty but untouchable. I prepare a bowl of fresh fruit—organic if I can find it. If I can't find organic fruit, I buy the freshest fruit I can get and give it a vinegar bath. I soak the fruit for ten minutes in a dishpan of lukewarm water to which I add one quarter cup of vinegar and then I rinse it in clear water and dry it. This vinegar bath, it is said, will remove up to 80 percent of the superficial sprays. You can never remove the spray which the plant has absorbed systemically.

Hospitalized people usually suffer with constipation and they welcome any natural help they can get. I once brought a gift-wrapped can of tenderized prunes to a little old lady of whom I am very fond. She told me later that while the other patients were submitting to enemas and laxatives, her regularity was the envy of the ward. "The prunes did it," she

said. "I ate two every night before going to sleep."

If my hospitalized friend has had surgery, I always bring a jar of sprouts. This may seem like an unorthodox gift. Perhaps it is. I include a note which says "I could have brought you a beautiful box of candy—but I love you so I didn't. I brought you these alfalfa sprouts instead."

Alfalfa sprouts are a terrific source of vitamin K, which is essential for the coagulation or clotting of blood. Recently it was found that hospitalized patients are deficient in this factor. Dr. J. Hirsch reported in the *Canadian Medical Association Journal,* November 3, 1973, that serious unexpected bleeding occurred in 27 patients during the early postoperative period and that this bleeding was due to vitamin K deficiency.

What is even more alarming is that the investigators concluded that the vitamin K deficiency developed during the patients' hospitalization.

Why did these patients develop this deficiency? The doctors attributed this rapid onset of vitamin K deficiency to poor food intake and frequent use of antibiotics.

Most hospitals do not routinely test for such nutrient levels, so it is difficult to estimate the frequency of vitamin K deficiency. The doctor strongly recommended that patients on limited oral food intake and patients treated with antibiotics receive supplemental vitamin K prior to undergoing surgery. In addition to supplements, they recommended including in the diet foods rich in vitamin K—green, leafy vegetables, like spinach, broccoli, kale, turnip or mustard greens. Not many hospital kitchens serve these greens regularly.

Alfalfa sprouts are one of the richest sources of vitamin K. They can be eaten in the raw, which means they also contribute factors which Dr. Roger Williams says contribute to super nutrition.

Sometimes, for the sake of variety, interest, and super nutrition, I bring a sprout sampler—a basket of little jars which contain wheat, alfalfa, rye, mung beans, chick-peas and garbanzos—all sprouted. People with health problems need not be afraid to eat sprouts. On the contrary, the starch and the protein of sprouts are readily digested because of the high quantity of enzymes they contain. All sprouts contain vitamins A, B and C equivalent to that found in fruit. Alfalfa sprouts are also rich in vitamins D, E, K, riboflavin and vitamin U, which has been found an effective aid against ulcers. Chick-pea sprouts are delicious and are especially high in protein.

Another presentation I sometimes make is my famous snick-snack platter. It is a nutritious delight. Halvah, Carob Nut Fudge, Carrot Coconut Cake, Peanut Butter Confections—all beautifully arranged to tempt the most picky eater and to satisfy anyone's sweet tooth. They are all made without a grain of sugar, white flour or hydrogenated fats.

Another of my favorite offerings is Ambrosia Cream for which I gave the recipe in my book *Confessions of a Sneaky Organic Cook*, but in case you don't have it, it's included with the recipes at the end of this chapter. I have never seen anyone who was able to resist it. I like to bring this to patients who are on antibiotics because it is made with yogurt which helps to establish the friendly bacteria which the antibiotics knock out of the colon.

If you must be admitted to the hospital as a patient, there are steps which you can take to make your stay a short and reasonably pleasant one.

If you must have surgery, you can take steps to minimize the dangers associated with the postoperative period.

Surgery always involves hazards. One of the gravest of these is deep vein thrombosis, a formation of blood clots in the veins, usually in the calves of the legs. One of every 200 persons undergoing major surgery dies—not from the surgery but from the venous blood clot which took a trip to his lungs.

What causes this life-threatening deep vein thrombosis? When the body suffers any kind of wound (and surgery is a wound), blood produces a chemical which accelerates the clotting time and thereby slows down the bleeding rate at the site of the wound. But, it also slows down the blood in the circulatory system. Blood is returned to the lungs for oxygenation and thence to the heart partly by pressure generated by movement of the legs and a series of valves in the veins. When a person is immobilized, as is usually the case after surgery, this return flow slows down, which increases the tendency of blood to coagulate in the leg veins.

135

There is another theory. Many physicians and surgeons believe that the surgical patient who develops deep vein thrombosis is suffering from a deterioration of the veins, a condition which causes rough inner surfaces to which coagulating blood clings, forming the dangerous clots.

This theory prompted English pathologist, Dr. Constance Spittle, to try vitamin C as a deterrent to the formation of pulmonary embolisms. Because vitamin C is vital to the health of the capillary system and the arteries, Dr. Spittle reasoned that vitamin C may well be important to the health of the veins. She set out to test her theory with a double blind trial. Using vitamin C (one thousand milligrams a day) and a placebo, she developed a trial in which the distribution among patients was structured by the hospital pharmacist so that nobody involved in the study had any knowledge of who was getting what.

Either the vitamin or placebo was administered before surgery and continued daily until two weeks after the operation. The results were tremendous.

When the code was broken, it was found that 30 patients had been given the vitamin C, while 33 had received the placebo. In the placebo group, 60 percent had developed thrombosis. In the vitamin C group 33 percent had some thrombotic development, or just about half as many as in the other group. Moreover, ten patients in the placebo group had double thrombosis, that is, clots in both legs, whereas none of the patients in the vitamin C group were thrombotic to that extent. Of the placebo patients three ultimately developed pulmonary embolisms. Of the vitamin C group none were bothered by this after-effect, which is really the most tragic result of the blood clot.

Dr. Spittle goes on to say in her article, which appeared in the British medical journal *Lancet*, July 28, 1973, "It is now six months since the trial was completed. Since that time some of our general and orthopedic surgeons are giving 500 milligrams of vitamin C to their patients daily. During this period in six wards we had a total of three cases of clinical deep vein trombosis and three of pulmonary embolism (two slight). "I am now recommending that the dose be increased to one gram daily."

A different and perhaps even more successful approach to the same problem has been developed in the United States and in Canada. That approach is to use a vitamin which will prevent thrombosis from developing in the first place—vitamin E. Dr. Alton Ochsner of New Orleans, one of this country's most distinguished surgeons, has been using vitamin E with outstanding success. Dr. Ochsner said in a letter to the *New England Journal of Medicine* (July 23, 1964) that since he has been using vitamin E he has not had one single case of pulmonary embolism. In all patients in whom venous thrombosis might develop he routinely prescribes alpha-tocopherol 100 I.U.'s three times a day until his patient is completely ambulatory. "Alpha-tocopherol," (vitamin E) he says, "is a potent inhibitor of thrombin that does not produce a hemorrhagic tendency and therefore is a safe prophylactic against venous thrombosis...the prophylactic treatment is generally simple and safe."

Dr. Wilfrid E. Shute says in his book, *Vitamin E for Ailing and Healthy Hearts*, that he and his brother Evan, of the Shute Clinic in London, Ontario, use vitamin E to treat coronary thrombosis. They only occasionally have a case of thrombosis in the legs and their patients simply do not have any pulmonary embolisms.

Unless your doctor is one of the new breed of physicians who is aware of what vitamins can do, he probably won't suggest that you take vitamins C and E prior to surgery or afterwards. Pharmaceutical companies don't promote vitamins aggressively for such purposes, so chances are that your doctor doesn't know. Most doctors shy away from vitamin treatment anyway for fear others in the profession may label them faddist and they will then suffer a loss of status. However, if they should lose a patient because of pulmonary embolism, they know that none of their colleagues would raise an eyebrow.

Since you cannot rely on your doctor to advise you to protect yourself with vitamin E and vitamin C, you will have to rely on yourself. Be sure you are well-fortified with both of these vitamins before you go to the hospital, while you're there and for at least a couple of weeks after you leave. Remember that your normal needs for these antioxidants increases with age. Add to this the increased requirements of stress and do your arithmetic accordingly.

When my husband was scheduled for an ear operation,

he tripled his daily vitamin intake for one week prior to surgery. He suffered no nausea nor any of the traumatic effects of surgery that brought misery to most of the other patients who had the same procedure.

Vitamins E and C are not the only ones which can shorten your stay in the hospital and increase your chances of survival.

Adelle Davis in *Let's Get Well* suggests a preparatory period of one month before surgery—especially for anyone who has been quite ill. During the preparatory period, put the stress on protein foods and every day eat six small meals which supply at least 25 grams of protein each. Good sources of protein are fresh, whole milk or skim milk fortified with powdered milk, nutritional yeast, soy flour, meat, fish, cheese, eggs, yogurt, custard or cereals cooked in milk. Yogurt or acidophilus milk help to destroy gas-forming intestinal bacteria. To get those nutrients which are not readily obtainable from foods, increase your intake of supplements. Particularly important are vitamins C, B₂ and pantothenic acid. B₆ too is very important, especially to those who are subject to nausea and vomiting.

Sometimes this kind of preparation for surgery improves a patient's health so much that surgery becomes unnecessary. Miss Davis says that her files contain dozens of such reports: A woman whose bursitis cleared up while she was preparing for an operation on her shoulder; several people whose hemorrhoids disappeared; others whose kidney stones, gall stones or prostates stopped causing trouble and even a woman whose inflamed uterus cleared up.

Adelle Davis suggests this "nightcap" the evening before surgery: 1,000 milligrams of vitamin C, 500 milligrams of pantothenic acid, 20 milligrams of B_2 and B_6, 2,500 milligrams of vitamin D, 300 units of vitamin E, and 500 milligrams of calcium lactate. This latter will encourage rapid clotting and prevent unnecessary bleeding. I know of an 80 year-old woman who took this nightcap before abdominal surgery and also took large doses of vitamins after her operation. Her progress was so good that her doctor was amazed and cited her case as an example of his own skill. (He never knew that she had taken these vitamins).

Have a "sweet" evening the night before surgery.

Some physicians prescribe lemonade loaded with sugar to be taken throughout the day before surgery. But Adelle Davis points out that if many hours intervene between the intake of the sugar and the surgery, much of the sugar is changed into fat. So limit your sweet intake to the night before you are scheduled for an operation.

After surgery, don't just lie there. Get right up on your feet as soon as your doctor will allow you to. Dr. David Shuman of Philadelphia told an American Osteopathic Association meeting that patients put on their feet as quickly as possible usually recover faster—and have fewer side effects—than those who stay in bed. Those who are put on a regimen of prolonged rest often gain little more than a whole

140

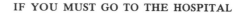

new set of complications, Dr. Shuman said.

Another thing which you should do if you are hospitalized is to spruce up. At one time little attention was given to a patient's appearance. He could lie there with his nightshirt rumpled up like a laundry bag and his hair a sparrow's nest. And no one thought of taking a female patient to the beautician to have her hair done.

Then doctors and nurses began to discover that patients have a higher motivation to get well and return to productive pursuits if they look well.

Today, in more enlightened institutions, especially for the elderly, patients are provided with bed clothes in cheerful pastel colors. A barber comes around to shave the men daily. There is usually a beauty parlor on the premises and Gray Ladies will take women to get facials and hairdos.

Because how you feel is influenced by how you look and how others tell you you look, do a little primping, fix your hair and your face and you will look a lot better to yourself and to your guests.

While you are in the hospital insist on your rights as an individual. There is no law that says you must take any medication without knowing what it is and why it was ordered for you. When my husband had his operation, a night nurse brought him some pills and he asked what they were.

"They were ordered by your doctor," the nurse answered.

"What are they for?" he insisted.

"I don't know," she said, "they were ordered by your doctor."

"I don't care who ordered them," my husband said, "I will not take any medicine unless I know what it is."

The nurse left in a huff and returned 15 minutes later and said, "They're to make you sleep."

"Thank you very much," my husband replied. "I do not need anything to make me sleep." And he did not take them.

Sometimes, if your bowels are not moving, the doctor will order a laxative—sometimes mineral oil. Mineral oil takes the oil soluble vitamins out of your body before your body has had a chance to utilize them and you are in a weakened state and subject to infection. One of the oil soluble vitamins which does a fast getaway is vitamin A, the anti-infection vitamin. In your weakened state you need every defense that you can muster. If the prunes have not succeeded in keeping your bowels open, then instead of a laxative, insist on an enema. It will be less destructive to your body's defense system.

Be sure to take a jar of wheat germ and some brewer's yeast to the hospital with you. Instead of the dry cereals which the hospital kitchen provides, have wheat germ and fruit with milk for your breakfast. Instead of coffee or tea fix yourself a cup of yeast broth.

Follow these suggestions and you will be out of the hospital before the nurses have learned how to spell your name.

Halvah

½ cup coconut (unsweetened, shredded)
½ cup sunflower seeds
½ cup wheat germ
¼ cup tahini (ground sesame seed)
¼ cup raw honey

1. Grind the coconut, sunflower seeds and wheat germ in a seed mill.

2. Put in a medium-sized mixing bowl and add tahini and honey. Mix together to form a dough-like consistency.

3. Separate dough into two portions. Place each portion on a piece of parchment or wax paper and form into a one-inch roll. Wrap tightly in the paper and keep in the refrigerator.

4. Cut into one-inch pieces as needed.

Carob Nut Fudge

I always take these to cardiac patients because they are so good for the heart. Carob powder is rich in potassium which is your heart's best friend and very low in sodium, which can be an enemy to your heart. Because these confections contain soy grits they are loaded with lecithin, which helps to dissolve cholesterol. Sesame seeds provide calcium, another element which is essential to heart health. Sunflower seeds and the wheat germ abound in many vitamins and minerals that are not found in the usual all-American diet. This Carob fudge, even though it is a delicious confection, actually has an excellent balance of amino acids making these confections a good protein food.

½ cup carob powder
½ cup raw honey
½ cup sesame seeds
½ cup wheat germ
¼ cup soy grits or soy powder
½ cup shredded coconut

In a large bowl mix all the ingredients, except coconut, together to make a ball of dough. Sprinkle half of the coconut on the bottom of a 9 x 9 pyrex dish. Press the ball into this dish filling in the four corners. Sprinkle remaining coconut on top and press it into the fudge with the bottom of a glass. Refrigerate briefly, then cut into small squares.

Peanut Butter Confections

1 cup natural peanut butter (not hydrogenated)
½ cup raw honey
1 teaspoon pure vanilla extract
¾ cup sunflower seed meal (put sunflower seeds in
      seed mill or blender to make the meal)
1 cup oatmeal (not instant)
⅓ cup sesame seeds
¼ cup finely-chopped walnuts or pecans for
      coating

1. In a large bowl, combine peanut butter, honey and vanilla extract.

2. Add next three ingredients. If the mixture is stiff, add two tablespoons of boiling water.

3. Roll the balls in finely-chopped nuts.

4. Refrigerate the balls until you are ready to use them.

When I assemble the confections on a tray, I cut some of them in half and arrange these half moons around the edge of the tray.

Carrot Coconut Cake

1 cup grated raw carrots
¾ cup coconut crumbs
½ cup raw honey or maple syrup
1 teaspoon pure vanilla extract
6 eggs
1 cup raw cashews (ground)
¾ teaspoon cream of tartar

1. In a large mixing bowl, blend carrots, coconut crumbs and honey. Add vanilla to carrot mixture and blend.

2. Separate the eggs. Beat the egg yolks to a creamy consistency.

3. Fold the egg yolks into the carrot and coconut mixture. Let it stand for at least one hour or until it has soaked up the moisture.

4. Add the ground nuts and blend.

5. Beat the egg whites until stiff. Then sprinkle cream of

tartar over them and mix it in. Fold the egg whites into the other ingredients.

6. Pour batter into angel food cake pan (ungreased).

Bake at 350° for 45 minutes. When cake tests done, turn the pan upside down on a rack until cake is cool.

Ambrosia Cream

1 pint sour cream
1 pint yogurt
Crushed pineapple (unsweetened)
½ cup walnuts
½ cup coconut (unsweetened)
1 pound of seedless grapes
2 oranges

Drain pineapple. Peel and section oranges. Mix all ingredients together. Garnish with a few orange sections. Add a little honey, or any good natural jam sweetened with honey, if you need a little more sweetness. Let the flavors meld in the refrigerator for a few hours before serving.

Bye-Bye Blues

How's your disposition today? Are you bursting at the seams with good cheer, vitality, good will? Do you feel like you could dance a jig, clean out the closets, mastermind a fund raising campaign, chair a board meeting, jog around the block, write a sonnet?

Or, do you feel plain rotten? Are you unable to cope? Fearful, apprehensive, cranky, moody, depressed? If you are in the second category, move over, you have plenty of company.

Depression with its side-kicks, lethargy and lack of energy, is one of the most common diseases in the world. And it is one of the main reasons why countless numbers of people are hooked on pills ("up" pills and "down" pills).

Doctors in the United States wrote more than 220 million prescriptions in 1970 for mood-altering drugs. Today, one out of every three Americans admits to their use and women users outnumber men two to one, reports Roland Berg (*McCalls*, September, 1971).

By this time, most of us are aware that these drugs are bad news. They lead to addiction, to serious side effects and they cure *nothing*.

True, some doctors hand them out like lemon drops and we tend to feel that anything that we get from our physician can be gulped down with safety. But, according to Berg's study, doctors are being duped by the persuasive advertising claims spread over the pages of scientific journals. Even more incriminating, according to one doctor, is the basic ignorance on the part of the medical profession of dangerous medicines and their complicated side effects.

Let's face it, drugs cannot offer any real solution to the problems of living. The discoverer of the tranquilizer Miltown, Dr. Frank M. Burger, president of Wallace Laboratories, told a health forum in Brooklyn that people looking for a lift should not take tranquilizers. "In spite of popular opinion," he said, "patients feel much worse after taking tranquilizers than before." Tranquilizers are useful in treating certain mental illnesses, he added, but they are not "happy pills."

Is there such a thing as a happy pill? Not really. But, take heart. There is much magic that you can conjure in your kitchen that will bring you a sense of super

148

well-being and a heavy dose of inner peace.

Once you learn the magic foods, you can manipulate the menu at your house to make sure that all the elements that nourish the *psyche* as well as the *soma* are bountiful in your meals and snacks.

For example, blood sugar levels that yo-yo from high to low and back again, frequently cause nervousness, irritability, depression, forgetfulness, insomnia, constant worrying, mental confusion, compulsive drinking of alcoholic beverages, lack of sexual drive and nervous breakdowns. It is estimated that there are 20 million Americans suffering with low blood sugar and don't know it. Many of them are horizontal on psychiatric couches when they should be vertical at the dinner table because their troubles can be cured simply with proper diet, says nutritionist Carlton Fredericks in his book, *Low Blood Sugar and You* (Constellation International, 1969).

A well-known New York psychiatrist insists on a six-hour glucose tolerance test to rule out the presence of hypoglycemia (low blood sugar) before he does any counseling. He has found that many times what his tired, depressed, emotionally disturbed, neurotic patient desperately needs is not a session on the couch—but a change of diet.

He recommends high protein (lean meat, eggs, fish), moderate fat (predominantly of the polyunsaturated type) and low carbohydrates. He allows no white sugar or white flour products.

When you have low blood sugar, your brain is being starved for glucose which is its chief food. That is why the control of the levels of glucose in your blood is so important to your mental and physical health. If your brain is getting too little glucose, as is the case with hypoglycemia, it is starving. It cannot function so you feel exhausted, miserable and ravenous for something sweet. The sweet will give you a quick pick-up and a major let-down. When you have hypoglycemia, your pancreas is over-active, and every time you eat sugars, it sends a rush of insulin into your bloodstream. The insulin removes all the sugar from your bloodstream and you are worse off than you were before.

Your cravings can be better controlled if you eat frequent meals—five or six small ones—instead of three large ones. By eating often, you eat less each time so that instead of having three wide upward and downward swings in blood sugar levels, you will have six or seven narrow ones. In time, the level tends to smooth out. Small meals are better utilized by the body. They minimize conversion of food into fat and actually help you to lose weight. They also lessen the desire to nibble on forbidden foods.

We consume far too many empty calorie foods—foods without protein, minerals, vitamins—just fillers. Not only do these foods contain no vitamins, they rob our personal vitamin bank accounts. Sugar, for instance, needs B vitamins in order to be metabolized. Having none of its own, it borrows yours—and *never pays them back.*

The B complex vitamins are absolutely essential to the

health of your nerves. A doctor friend of mine braces himself for a night of socializing by taking a couple of B-complex vitamin tablets before he goes out. The liquor he imbibes doesn't take such a disastrous toll when he is thus fortified.

Empty-calorie, junk foods place you in double jeopardy. They not only gobble up your vitamins, they displace the foods that would be giving you natural vitamins and minerals. And, maybe you didn't know it, but if your system is deprived of even a single food chemical, your mental state might suffer. You just don't feel "with it."

Perhaps it is not just an accident of genes that some people are perpetual sourpusses while others exude good humor and optimism—even people of the same family eating at the same table. One member of the family may be helping himself to doubles on mashed potatoes while another will double-up on the salads—one will reach for an apple, another for a doughnut or a candy bar.

Doctors are still advising, "Eat a balanced diet and you'll get all the food elements you need." This may have been true before our foods were refined, processed and adulterated with additives. It is not true today. And that is one big reason why so many of us, including doctors, are leading tired listless lives and living through blue Mondays every day of the week.

Let's consider the role pantothenic acid plays in the way you feel. This is one of the vitamins left on the milling room floor in the flour refining fiasco. Since we're not getting pantothenic acid from commercial bread or any product made of white flour, many of us are deficient in it.

When you lack pantothenic acid, you suffer the vague pains of neuritis, lack of energy, an inability to think clearly and lapses of memory. Pantothenic acid is the anti-stress vitamin and is number one on anyone's tranquility program.

In fact, with plenty of pantothenic acid in your blood, you are much better equipped to hit the boss for a raise, to say "No" to the kids, to face an audience, or to drive a car in traffic.

If you are doing heavy physical work, if you're facing surgery, if you have an infection, you may need twice as much pantothenic acid as you usually do, says Dr. I. Scorady in *Acta Paediat. Hung.* (1963).

You would be wise to increase your pantothenic acid intake if you have a color tv, or if you are anticipating x-ray studies of any part of your body, if you are taking antibiotics or if you have any kind of allergic manifestation.

All of these conditions, and many more, create stress. And pantothenic acid is perhaps your best defense against stress of all kinds. While this vitamin is important to every cell of your body, its tremendous assist in situations of stress is due to its essential contribution to the smooth function of your adrenal glands. Without pantothenic acid, adrenal glands just don't express their usual "fight or flight" reaction. In fact, a lack of pantothenic acid can cause your adrenal glands to go on strike, to lay down on the job and refuse to produce cortisone and other important hormones.

Without these hormones, you just cannot operate on all cylinders, and you're particularly vulnerable to any situation that causes stress. And, as we all know, life is made of stressful situations.

To sustain a cheerful disposition, you should get between five and 10 milligrams of pantothenic acid daily. Wheat germ is an excellent source of it. Liver is also abundant in pantothenic acid (about five milligrams in one-quarter pound or an average serving). Other good meat sources are kidney, heart, spleen, brain, pancreas (sweetbreads) and tongue. Muscle meats (steaks and roasts) are lowest.

Pantothenic acid is in many of the same foods that contain the other B vitamins—nutritional yeast, egg yolk, peanuts, rice bran or brown rice, broccoli, salmon, soybeans.

There must be something on tonight's dinner menu that you can enrich with a good source of pantothenic acid. Are you making soup? Add two heaping tablespoons of powdered or flaked yeast just before you serve it. It will enhance the flavor and help to improve everyone's disposition.

Another nutrient that helps you put on a happy face is niacin (vitamin B_3). A poor sense of humor may be caused by a niacin deficiency.

We have known for many years that complete lack of niacin causes pellagra, a disease characterized by severe depression, reminiscent of schizophrenia. Dr. Abram

Hoffer, eminent psychiatrist and director of psychiatric research for Saskatchewan's Department of Public Health, uses massive doses of niacin in treating schizophrenia. With it he has been able to rescue many patients from the "snake pit" of so-called incurables. Dr. Hoffer is convinced that a daily dose of at least one gram of vitamin B_3 for everyone would result in a significant decrease in the incidence of schizophrenia.

Niacinamide, a buffered form of niacin, appears to be non-toxic in any quantity. (It is far safer than aspirin.) Dr. Hoffer uses it to reduce high cholesterol and fat levels in the blood, as well as a treatment for schizophrenia and other mental ills. He tells of giving one mental patient 1,000 milligrams of this vitamin every hour for 40 hours, after which time she was well and remained so. Niacin alone usually causes the skin to become red, flushed and prickly for perhaps an hour after it is taken. To avoid this kind of reaction take the niacinamide.

The amount of niacinamide needed by different individuals varies widely. Adelle Davis reports that for years she obtained excellent results with only 100 milligrams taken after each meal, always with brewer's yeast, liver, or other natural sources of the vitamin B's. She now recommends 100 milligrams of niacinamide daily for adolescents and college students under severe stress (*Let's Eat Right to Keep Fit,* Harcourt, Brace, Jovanovich).

The house physician at our local hospital, who takes the histories and performs the physicals on new patients, tells me that she is amazed at the increasing number of patients who show signs of vitamin deficiencies—especially the patients in the psychiatric ward. "But," she says, "it is almost impossible to convince the patient's doctor that this is the case. 'Mrs. Winslow, deficient in vitamin B? Impossible! She's a rich woman!' " Vitamin deficiency is no respector of bank books.

Do you begin to see the parts of the puzzle fitting together? Any nutrient relieves the symtoms caused by its lack. If niacin can help to cure schizophrenia, it should be effective in preventing it. If a severe niacin shortage can cause schizophrenia, a mild deficiency may cause blue Mondays, depression, gloom, mental confusion. Even a cheerful, pleasant, optimistic person may become tired, apprehensive, and pessimistic when his body's need for niacin is not being met.

Niacin is another one of the B vitamins which lands on the milling room floor during the refining process. The so-called enrichment program restores one-third of the original amount. Isn't it ridiculous that it was removed in the first place?

In what foods do you find niacin? One of the best sources is yeast. I'm talking about brewer's yeast—not baking yeast. There's a big difference. Uncooked baker's yeast contains live yeast plant cells, great for raising bread, but a threat to unassimilated B-complex vitamins in your body. The yeast plants are killed by heat during the baking process and, once killed, can no longer play havoc with your digestive tract.

Brewer's yeast, sometimes called nutritional yeast, is, on the other hand, a rich storehouse of human nutrition, a good natural source of minerals, enzymes, proteins and all the B vitamins. One quarter of a cup of the brewer's yeast gives you 100 milligrams of the niacin. It contains practically no fat, starch or sugar.

Because it is an excellent protein, brewer's yeast sticks to the ribs, satisfies the appetite, improves metabolism and provides the vigor and temperament to tackle jobs you've been pushing aside. It's a great reducing food, helps to keep blood sugar levels on an even keel, and because it is an excellent source of niacin and thiamin (vitamin B_1—another insulator of nerve endings), it is the kind of a mood elevator whose only side effect is a nice, warm inner glow.

If you have been subject to crying spells for no reason at all, look to your thiamin (B_1) intake just as a safety precaution. A person who is deficient in B_1 lacks energy and is constantly tired. He neither eats well nor sleeps well, and he tends to be cross and irritable.

Much of the irritability in people who give you a hard time at shopping centers or on the highway might be traced to a deficiency in this essential nutrient. "Many groups do not receive adequate amounts of thiamin," says Miriam E. Lowenberg in *Food and Man* (John Wiley and Sons, Inc., 1968). "Often dietary lack of thiamin is not so great as to cause definite illness, but the intake is not enough for good health."

Mood changes are sometimes the first indication that this vitamin is lacking and this signal, if heeded, can help you avoid changes in your brain—some of them irreversible. If your memory has become faulty and your concentration span is poor, start immediately to increase your B₁ intake. If you feel unstable emotionally and overreact to the normal stresses and strains of everyday living, if you blow a fuse at the slightest provocation, these are some of the red lights warning of danger ahead.

Fortunately, except in cases of extreme organic damage, thiamin therapy usually brings dramatic recoveries, even after the deficiency has advanced to the stage of beriberi (the name given to extreme thiamin deficiency many years ago). Back in the 1890's, Dr. Christian Eijkman found he could give chickens polyneuritis (beriberi in man) by restricting them to a diet of polished rice. He could reverse the process and cure them when he fed them natural, unprocessed brown rice. That's a clue for you. Never use processed rice. Brown rice is inexpensive, easy to prepare, delicious and rich in this "morale" vitamin. "The cereal grains are good sources of thiamin," Dr. Lowenberg says, "but the thiamin is in the germ and outer coatings so that refined cereals such as white rice and flour have lost their thiamin."

Bear in mind that there are other factors which contribute to a thiamin deficiency. This vitamin is soluble in water (the more water you use in cooking, the more thiamin you lose). It is destroyed by high temperatures and by some chemicals, including baking soda.

Your body's need for thiamin varies under different circumstances. Dr. Myron Brin writing in *Newer Methods of Nutritional Biochemistry* (Academic Press, 1967), says we need extra supplies of the vitamin during the use of antibiotics, in the case of severe diarrhea and "in any other situation that would affect adversely the absorption or utilization of the nutrient."

If you are facing surgery or a big day at the office, or even a happy event—like your daughter's wedding or anticipating the birth of a grandchild—these are stressful conditions that call for more thiamin. If the love of your life is struggling with an income tax return, he will be much more cheerful about it if he has plenty of thiamin working for him. Put out a dish of *sunflower seeds* for him to snack on. Seeds are a wonderful source of all the B vitamins. Everytime you have a birthday, increase your daily allotment of thiamin and you will be holding back the manifestations of the aging process. Your need for thiamin increases with your birthdays. The Committee on Foods and Nutrition of the National Research Council recommends 1.5 milligrams a day for a sedentary man and 2.3 milligrams for one who is very active. This much will keep you from getting beriberi. But you need much more for optimum well being—mental as well as physical.

One of the most exciting possibilities concerning thiamin is that more than just enough can improve mental ability. In an experiment conducted by Dr. Ruth F. Harrell of

the Department of Educational Psychology at Columbia University, two groups of children in an orphanage, who ranged in age from 9 to 19, were closely matched in age, sex, weight, educational status, and mentality. One group was given a daily tablet containing two milligrams of thiamin; the other group received a placebo. It was a double blind experiment—to insure objectivity, the children did not know which pills they were receiving, and neither did the investigators. This procedure was continued for a year. Only after all the results were in did Dr. Harrell and her associates match up the testing scores to see how the vitamin group performed compared to the placebo group.

Several categories of tests were used, each designed to measure an aspect of mental response. Both groups were tested at the beginning of the experiment and again at the end, and their percentage of improvement compared with a control group. The group which received the thiamin supplements showed astonishing improvement in all categories—as much as 25 percent to 3,200 percent. "It appears," say Drs. E. Cheraskin, W. M. Ringsdorf and J. W. Clark, in *Diet and Disease* (Rodale Books, 1968), "that mental achievement of children of presumably normal diet can be remarkably increased through employment of dietary supplements."

Mental alertness, then, like emotional stability, serenity, and even pleasant disposition and a zest for living, has been shown to suffer when dietary intake of thiamin is low. With plenty of thiamin, your morale hits new highs and you enjoy that wonderful feeling of being able to cope with whatever life may bring.

The foods that are rich in thiamin are also rich in all the other B-complex vitamins. You should get your thiamin as a part of the B complex in a natural compound—brewer's yeast, desiccated liver and wheat germ—the trio that can change your life.

An undersupply of several other nutrients can affect your personality, your charisma, and the way you face each day. If you are even mildly deficient in the mineral magnesium, you are apt to be highly nervous, irritable, quick to pick a quarrel, uncooperative, withdrawn, surly, apathetic or belligerent.

Tip to mothers, and grandmothers, when the children are "impossible:" put out a dish of sunflower seeds, raw almonds and raw cashews—all high in magnesium. I don't know whether it's because their jaws are so busy or because the magnesium is going to work, but somehow this little repast seems to have a magical effect on rambunctious dispositions. According to Dr. Willard A. Krehl, magnesium deficiency unquestionably causes changes in nerve conduction, transmission at the myoneuro junction and muscular contraction (*Nutrition Today,* September 1967). The British medical journal, *Lancet,* reports that a case of mental apathy and depression was caused by a thiamin deficiency which in turn was caused by a magnesium deficiency (October 1, 1966).

In addition to nuts, foods that are rich in magnesium

are dolomite, bone meal, some meats, eggs, fruits, and vegetables. (Organically grown fruits and vegetables absorb chelated trace minerals from the humus-enriched soil. This does not happen when synthetic fertilizers are used).

Perhaps the mineral which most helps to control nervous tension and irritability is calcium. In fact, whenever you feel the need of a tranquilizer take calcium instead. I use the bone meal because it has other minerals, such as phosphorus and magnesium, that work with the calcium.

Dr. John Wozny, psychiatrist at the Department of Educational Psychology of the University of Alberta, finds that calcium beats psychotherapy for effectiveness in solving many problems. One of his patients, a young girl of 13, was beset with tensions that made it difficult for her to make friends. Insomnia plagued her every night and the fatigue which resulted compounded her nervousness. Taking a test at school was torture. All her tensions, apprehensions and irritability developed into a constant morbid fear. Dr. Wozny had seen research indicating that there is an excessive rise in the lactate levels (lactate is a normal metabolic product) in patients with anxiety neurosis. He knew that calcium binds with lactate, thereby neutralizing it. He put Mary on a high calcium diet. "Twenty-three days later," he reports, "great improvement was noted...Mary indicated that she felt better, had managed to overcome some peer group problems in school, was getting a full night's sleep, and had managed to reach the point where she had a downright willingness to enter into school test situations."

This theory was put to the test again on 14-year-old Larry, who had anxiety problems with a long history of ineffective therapy. His condition was coupled with a nagging pain in the muscles of the neck, which Dr. Wozny believed was due to his highly-nervous state. Once on a high calcium diet, however, Larry's work in school began to improve. His neck felt much better and eventually the stiffness disappeared.

But Larry inadvertently went even further to demonstrate the effectiveness of a high calcium diet. "After 23 high-calcium days," Dr. Wozny reports, "it seems Larry came to doubt the relative effectiveness of what was going on, and applied good scientific principles to his problem. Without telling anyone, he went off his diet to see if what we had been doing was just chemical nonsense. I saw him in my office on the 26th day, and Larry was a very chagrined young man. His stiff neck had come back with a vengeance. A hasty return to the calcium regimen restored a trouble-free muscular condition." Larry and Dr. Wozny were both most impressed.

When you understand how calcium exerts its almost magical tranquilizing effect, you will comprehend much more clearly the important interdependence between the *soma* and *psyche.* You can see how ridiculous it is to attempt to treat the mind without concern for the problems that affect the body.

Scientists have shown that it is an excess of lactate in

body chemistry that causes much of the anxiety, the nervousness and irritability, the tension and fears that plague so many of us today. Lactic acid is a normal product of glucose metabolism. In the normal course of events, lactic acid is not produced to any great extent. However, when energy must be produced fast, for example, when a runner sprints, when a writer pushes a deadline or when a housewife pushes a vacuum cleaner, the cells in the body undergo a process of metabolizing glucose and producing energy without using oxygen. This metabolism of glucose under anaerobic (airless) conditions is termed glycolosis, and the end product of glycolosis is lactate. When the lactate builds up, the result is fatigue. It is inevitable, therefore, that there will be lactate in your blood at periods of heavy exertion or simple muscle tension. When you have high levels of lactate, you have problems. But if plenty of calcium is available, the lactate will not have its unpleasant effects on your nervous system.

Besides bone meal, a very good source of calcium is the crunchy little sesame seed. According to the *Agricultural Handbook No. 34*, as little as one-quarter pound of sesame seeds gives you 1,125 milligrams of calcium. Besides being a powerhouse of calcium, sesame seeds are a wonderful source of the important B vitamins, protein and vitamin E, all necessary to your *joie de vivre*.

If you accentuate the positive and eliminate the negative you will become delightfully aware that you don't need up and down pills, tranquilizers, barbiturates, and the whole schmeer. You can get "high" on natural foods.

How to Stop
Counting Sheep

My mother summed up the age and insomnia paradox in one cogent sentence.

"When you're young enough to sleep, little children won't let you. When the children get older and let you sleep already, so you can't."

How I used to yearn for a few more minutes under the blanket in those days when the children were little and demanding immediate attention at the crack of dawn. Now that they are grown and snuggling under their own blankets, I frequently wake at the crack of dawn, edged out of slumberland by nothing more shattering than a sunbeam slipping through the window shade.

Early morning wakefulness is a phase of getting older

that I have learned to cope with—and enjoy. I don't fight it. I simply stretch, get up and get going. In fact, I have learned to love the early morning hours.

It's the wakefulness at the other end of the day that is particularly vexing to us as we get older. Many older people tend to doze off while watching tv, at movies, at plays, and even in the middle of a conversation. And then, when they hit the pillow, bingo, they're wide awake and counting sheep.

If you are one of the many older people who utter a fervent prayer for sleep as you turn down the lights, turn off the radio, set the alarm, and turn up the blanket, join the club. You are in the company of kings, artists, models, actors, scientists, overworked housewives and tired executives.

Insomnia has been termed the great undercover complaint of modern society. It has triggered massive drug taking and has led an army of hollow-eyed sufferers to the psychiatrist's couch. But don't despair. A simple change of snacks may pave the way to slumberland for you.

"Sleep that knits up the ravell'd sleave of care" can be an elusive balm and many so-called remedies have been extolled through the years. Every insomniac knows them by heart: relax like a jellyfish; think about black velvet; don't take worry into the bedroom; breathe deeply; try some yoga relaxation exercises; eat a snack before you go to bed; don't get overtired; avoid stress; exercise before going to bed; ventilate your room; and wear a nightshirt instead of pajamas.

Very little has been written about the kind of nutrition

that will promote a good night's sleep. There are some foods which help you relax and sleep and others that stimulate activity. Some foods shoot high octane into your bloodstream; others have a tranquilizing effect that help you slow down, turn off your motor, relax and sleep. You can't step on the gas and expect your car to stop.

Coffee is the chief enemy of sleep. Caffeine in any form stimulates the adrenals to produce more hormones, which send a message to the liver to get on the ball and break down that glycogen into glucose which flows into the bloodstream and makes you want to get up and go. This is why a cup of coffee "gives you a lift"—far away from the Land of Nod. Bear in mind that cocoa, tea, and soft drinks also contain caffeine and should be avoided like poison ivy if sleep is your objective.

Salt Is a Stimulant

While every insomniac knows about the wide-awake tossing he suffers in the still of the night because of unwise indulgence in caffeine, not many night tossers realize that a close runner-up to caffeine in the ranks of the sleep destroyers is salt—common everyday sodium chloride, the stuff you put in your soup, on your potatoes, tomatoes, eggs and radishes. If you eat the usual tv snacks such as pretzels, potato chips or salted nuts, you may be pushing sleep out the window.

When you stop to think about it, it isn't surprising that a

diet rich in salt should keep you awake nights. Salt is a stimulant. It is pointed out by Henry Bieler M. D., in his book *Food Is Your Best Medicine* (Random House, 1965), that salt stimulates the adrenal gland, just as caffeine does. In fact, salt is a two-time offender to the insomniac. It leads to high blood pressure which in itself is an enemy of restful sleep.

The usual medical treatment for high blood pressure is diuresis—administration of a drug which pulls the fluids from the tissues. Anyone who is on a diuretic can testify that sleep is frequently disturbed by an emergency call from the kidneys.

It makes far more sense to simply eliminate salt and not suffer from high blood pressure in the first place.

In the book *Sea of Life* (David McKay Co., 1969), Dr. William D. Snively reports a study of a large group of Americans questioned about the amount of salt they normally use. Out of 100 who reported that they never salt their food at the table, only one had high blood pressure; among 100 who said they add salt to taste, eight had high blood pressure; among 100 who said they add salt even before tasting, ten had high blood pressure. The doctors who worked on the study came to the conclusion that the most common form of high blood pressure or hypertension will not develop unless salt intake is excessive.

Why does excessive salt cause your pressure to go up, your blood to pound through your veins, your temples to throb so that you simply can't sleep? There is an old aphorism "Water goes where the salt is." Because sodium clings to water, when an excessive amount enters the extra-cellular fluid, it carries extra liquid with it. This naturally increases the volume of the plasma. In order to distribute the expanded blood, Dr. Snively explains, the heart must create additional pressure and therefore pumps harder. It is this pumping that has you counting sheep.

Sodium Fights Potassium

At a conference on mental hygiene, a French army doctor, Professor Ciorault, related insomnia to salt intake, pointing out that sodium and potassium are natural antagonists in the body's chemistry because a cell is in a state of repose when it is rejecting sodium and accepting potassium. It is in an active state when it is accepting sodium. He said he successfully cured his patients of sleeplessness simply by eliminating salt from their diets (*Salt and Your Health*, Hearthside Press, Inc., 1965).

A most interesting experiment was conducted by Dr. Michael Miller of St. Elizabeth Hospital in Washington, D. C., and reported in the *Journal of the American Medical Association* back in 1945 (September 22). Dr. Miller was able to help patients who had been getting only one and two hours of sleep a night. He didn't prescribe drugs or psychotherapy. He merely put his patients on a low-salt diet.

Seventeen of 20 patients, whose salt intake Dr. Miller had reduced to only two grams a day, started to sleep better almost at once and in three weeks reported happily that they were sleeping eight hours every night and waking up refreshed.

To make sure the effects were not just psychological, Dr. Miller restored salt to the diets of 13 of them without their knowledge. Within a few days ten of these patients were once again complaining of being tense, nervous and unable to sleep.

Remember that salt occurs in many foods that you have not salted. These are some of the foods on the forbidden list for those on a low salt diet:

Processed meats such as salted, smoked, canned, spiced and pickled meat, bacon, ham, sausage, bologna, shell fish (clams, oysters, lobsters, shrimp), all processed fish, frankfurters, liverwurst, salami, canned vegetables (unless specially packed without salt), beets, celery, endive, kale, spinach, sauerkraut, broths, meat soups, regular commercial bread and rolls, salted crackers, salted peanuts, pretzels, all processed cheeses, commercial ice cream and salted butter. Also forbidden are olives, ketchup, mayonnaise, pickles, relishes, salted meat gravy and salted meat sauce. Remember, too, that softened water has a high sodium content. If you must use a water softener, use it only on the hot water line. Use hard water for drinking and cooking.

Fruits, vegetables, cereals, fish and meat naturally provide all the vital food salts we need for our well-being. A 3½-ounce serving of salmon will give you 48 milligrams of sodium, 3½ ounces of turkey will give you 40 milligrams,

3½ ounces of chicken breasts will give you 78 and the same amount of chicken leg will give you 110 milligrams of sodium. This is without using the salt shaker. You get sodium in your vegetables. A cup of spinach gives you 164 milligrams; a cup of bects 220; carrots 62, turnip greens 20, dandelion 152, kale 220.

According to Dr. Snively, low sodium diets can range from 200 up to 1,000 milligrams a day. The average daily diet contains about 5,000 milligrams of sodium or from five to 25 times as much as is needed. No wonder so many people toss and turn instead of sleeping. It is interesting to note, Dr. Snively points out, that on these low-salt diets most people find that they miss salt less and less. Eventually, they may even develop a distinct distaste for it. No doubt, at that point they are sleeping like babies.

Foods That Aid Relaxation

Just as salt and caffeine are food substances that rev up your motor and prevent restful sleep, so there are some substances that have a peaceful tranquilizing effect and hasten your trip to the Land of Nod.

Chief among these tranquilizing substances is calcium.

A constant supply of calcium is required in the circulating blood for the building of bone and the control of electronic impulses transmitted through the nerves. If the concentration of calcium ions in the blood plasma falls below normal, the nerves lack the basic material that quiets them down. Muscle cells, as a result, often go into continuous contraction—this condition is known as tetany. Before the calcium deficit reaches the bankrupt stage that brings on tetany, you could experience what is commonly referred to as a case of nerves. No wonder you feel jumpy. Your nerve and muscle cells are screaming for calcium.

When you lie down to sleep, unless there is enough calcium in your bloodstream to meet the demands of your muscles and nerves, there won't be enough reaching your brain to shut off the constant "beep beep" signals that keep you awake. On the other hand, when your calcium supply is optimal, the blood delivers enough of it to satisfy all of your body's needs, the nervous system ceases to send out its frantic calls for calcium and you are on the train to slumberland.

The older you get the more calcium you need because your ability to absorb this mineral diminishes as the years pile up. This increased need for calcium in the latter years may be one reason why older people suffer from insomnia much more than younger people.

Don't be fooled into thinking that because you are getting less sleep with every birthday candle over 40, your need for sleep diminishes with age. Dr. Philip M. Tiller Jr., of the Louisiana State University School of Medicine believes that quite the contrary is true. In a study of 83 patients aged 60 and over who had been under observation for many years, it was found some patients slept much more than eight hours. The doctor believed that there had been an increase in their need for sleep with advancing age. Others whose sleep had decreased complained of insomnia and discomfort (*Modern Maturity*, December-January, 1971).

Patients who did not complain of insomnia but were, in fact, spending fewer hours between the covers seemed less tranquil and had more of the stigmata of old age than those who slept longer. It is probable that an increase in the consumption of calcium foods together with those food elements .which facilitate the metabolism of calcium, particularly vitamins A and D, would help you sleep more soundly and feel young longer.

How much calcium do you need to help you get to slumberland without counting sheep? Nutritionist Adelle Davis recommends two grams of calcium daily for anyone suffering from insomnia (*Let's Eat Right to Keep Fit*).

Make sure that your diet is enhanced with calcium-rich foods such as green leafy vegetables. Don't overlook seeds—especially sesame seeds which are extremely rich in calcium. Add some to tossed salads, coat liver or your hamburgers with sesame seeds; add the seeds to baked potatoes, fruit salads, hot vegetables. Use tahini (sesame butter) as a spread. Try mixing tahini with honey for a delicious snack that will encourage sound restful sleep.

Bone meal is an excellent calcium supplement to help you sleep soundly. It has the added advantage of a range of other minerals that help keep bones strong and sound.

One of these is magnesium which works in partnership with calcium and is absolutely essential to healthy nerves. Try bone meal powder in tomato juice, in baked goods or in homemade yogurt—the lactic acid facilitates its absorption. Add sesame seed and apple and you have another delicious, sleep-inducing snack to replace the salty ones that are keeping you awake.

There are other food elements which are absolutely vital to a good night's sleep.

If you aren't getting enough pantothenic acid you can be sleepy, yet have trouble falling asleep. This member of the B family, usually sold as calcium pantothenate, is most abundant in liver, kidney, heart, yeast, wheat germ and bran, whole grains and green vegetables. Because pantothenate acid is unstable to heat and thus destroyed in the canning or cooking process, Americans have been found woefully deficient in it. They get an average of three to five milligrams per day although the daily requirement appears to be more than 50 milligrams.

Another one of the B vitamins that is absolutely essential for a good night's sleep is B6. This vitamin often acts as a tranquilizer. Niacin, too, is necessary to a good night's sleep. Mushrooms are a good source of niacin, and so are heart, liver, wheat germ and brewer's yeast.

As for me, I take two bone meal and two dolomite tablets with 500 milligrams of vitamin C from rose hips. This facilitates absorption of the minerals. I am usually halfway to slumberland before I hit the pillow.

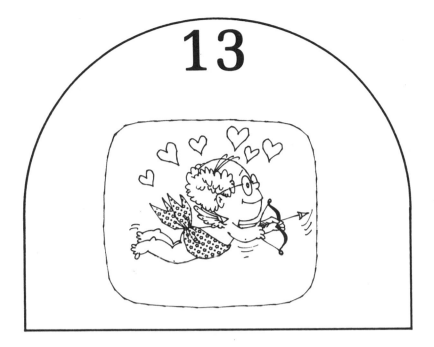

How Is Your Love Life?

How is your love life? I don't mean to be personal. But this is one of the areas which gerontologists (a fancy name for those scientists who try to find out what keep us old people ticking) are studying to determine what characteristics help us to live longer and enjoy it more.

An active sex life, it seems, not only adds considerable sparkle and enjoyment to your night life, but its afterglow actually increases the number of your days.

Do not put your sex life in mothballs just because you are getting older. It is just as appropriate in old age as in younger years, says Dr. Eric Pfeiffer in the *Journal of the American Geriatric Society*, 1972.

Consider that about 15,000 women and 35,000 men over

65 got married last year. As one gentleman so aptly put it, "Just because there's snow on the roof doesn't mean there's no fire in the furnace."

One of the most common fears, especially in men over 50, is that the stress of sex on their hearts could lead to a heart attack. Sex is a kind of a physical exercise and a person who is recovering from a heart attack should moderate this exercise as he would any other. But, Dr. Ewald W. Busse, Chairman of the Psychiatry Department of Duke University and Director of the Center for Aging and Human Development, pointed out a very important consideration when he addressed the American Medical Association in New York in July 1969. He said, abstaining from sex when it is desired is probably equally strenuous to the nervous system and the heart.

Sex can be pleasurable without being emotionally or physically strenuous, especially when it is enjoyed with a lifetime partner.

There are some precautions to take which apply to all ages, but especially to the elderly. If you've been partying and indulging in double-decker sandwiches and intoxicating liquids, you would be wiser to just simply conk out when you hit the pillow that night.

There is of course a natural slowing down process as we get older. It is important that men understand this and not push the panic button and think their ability to function sexually has disappeared. If they expect this to happen, their very expectations can make it happen. It is perfectly natural for the older man to respond more slowly to sexual impetus. If the slowing down of response results in a fear of performance, this fear itself can lead to impotence or a retreat from sexual interaction, according to Dr. Pfeiffer, Associate Professor of Psychiatry at Duke University.

It is important for wives to be aware of the physiological changes in men, Masters and Johnson advise, so they will not misinterpret their husbands' less frequent demands and slower response. Wives should not consider this a loss of capacity or a sign of diminishing affection.

On the distaff side, some women think that their sex life is over with menopause. Nothing could be farther from the truth. From a psychological standpoint, say Masters and Johnson, "There is no reason why the milestone of the menopause should be expected to blunt the human female's sexual capacity, performance, or drive."

There are some things which you can do naturally during the day which will greatly enhance the enchantment of your evenings. Vitamin E, which the Swedes call the sex vitamin, is practically lost to the American diet because of the manner in which our grains and oils are refined.

Vitamin E is vitally important, and has been much publicized, but it's only one of the nutrients needed for sexual harmony. Eat more live foods to bring a quality of aliveness to your glands. The healthy function of the endocrine glands, which secrete hormones, is indispensable to the healthy function of the sex organs.

What do your glands need to be healthy? They need

specific vitamins and minerals to function at top efficiency all through life. The refined food diet that's usual fare in the American home cannot possibly provide these nutrients. On the contrary, they can be harmful because they are bathed in chemical additives which destroy enzymes and contribute to the destruction of health and to the impairment of sexual strength, Dr. Paavo Airola points out in *Sex and Nutrition* (Information Inc., New York, 1970).

You cannot be really sensuous if you have an underactive thyroid gland. Nor can you hope to inspire a desire for sex in a hypothyroid partner. A weak or lazy thyroid does nothing for your sex life at any age. If you feel like a zombie when you get between the covers and want to do nothing but sleep, you may need more of the B vitamins and more iodine to nourish an underactive thyroid gland. Kelp is a good source of iodine. Use it instead of salt to season your food. To insure a good supply of the B vitamins, naturally, use brown rice, lots of wheat germ and nutritional yeast. Take a yeast break instead of a coffee break—mid-morning and mid-afternoon.

There are substances in peanuts, untoasted soy flour and vegetables of the cabbage family which combine with iodine and prevent it from reaching the blood, therefore causing a deficiency. Four milligrams of iodine daily, the amount in a teaspoon of kelp, is considered adequate to correct thyroid abnormalities. Since vitamin E improves iodine absorption and helps an underactive thyroid gland to produce hormones, you'll get more mileage out of your

178

iodine if you take it with your vitamin E. Put some wheat germ oil (rich in vitamin E) in a glass of tomato juice and spike it with a generous dash of kelp to get the combination.

The trace mineral zinc is called the mineral for men because the male reproductive system contains the highest concentration of zinc of any cells in the human body.

Zinc is sadly lacking in our diets. Like every other mineral element, zinc is concentrated in the bran and germ portion of the cereal grains which are removed in the refining process.

Another cause of zinc deficiency in the modern diet is current farming methods with their use of artificial fertilizers and poisonous insecticides. These have brought about a reduction in the amount of zinc in our food plants. This reduction is also transmitted to the cattle and other animals which we are consuming.

Green vegetables and nuts are good sources of zinc—especially if they are grown in healthy good soil. Zinc is lost when you consume excess liquids, particularly alcohol, or if any form of diuretic is being used. If your doctor has prescribed a diuretic, be sure you watch your zinc intake, and your potassium as well. Both minerals, along with many others, are depleted when you take a diuretic.

Perhaps your best source of zinc is seeds. Seeds are rich in the substances so necessary to new life and to the whole reproductive process. Pumpkin seeds, sunflower seeds, sesame seeds are excellent sources of zinc and should be included regularly in your diet. Throw away the usual snacks and instead serve a dish of mixed seeds and raisins. Garnish them with a little unsweetened coconut and you will have a snack that is rich in the nutrients your body needs to build new cells. If you sprout your seeds, you will multiply the values and benefits.

And that's not all. Because sprouts are alive, don't be surprised if you suddenly feel a new and wonderful quality of aliveness once you have incorporated them into your meal planning. You may even begin to have that wonderful feeling that you have stopped the aging process.

Years ago, Brown Landone reported on some experiments that were made on old decrepit rats. They were so old that, proportionately, they were about as old as a man 90 years. These decrepit old rats were fed what were then called "immature" foods. That is, foods which had not finished their growth, still in the act of sprouting new stems and very young leaves. The results were amazing. The decrepit old rats were transformed, and their bodies began to grow younger!

No one understood the cause of this phenomenon. The experiments had been conducted to test the effects of vitamins. But, with larger amounts of vitamins, using matured or full grown foods, the old rats did not grow younger. So the scientists realized that there was something other than vitamins, which worked like magic in growing youthful cells.

Several years passed and no one tumbled to the

significance of this experiment. Then, Mr. Landone began to experiment with younger growing plants, in this case the sprouts of bean seeds. He had used sprout foods for more than a generation but had no proof of what caused them to be of value.

At about the same time, other scientists discovered a root-auxin in plant roots. When they extracted this auxin from the tip of a young growing root, and pasted it on the edge of a leaf, roots grew even on the edge of the leaf! This, says Mr. Landone, is the miracle of auxinon foods. They induce growth after their own kind of activity. Root-auxin will grow roots. And a youth-auxinon will grow youthful cells.

Youth-growing substances from new growing sprouts will induce cells to grow younger, he says. That is, there is something in the chemical substances of a youth-growing auxinon which, when you eat it as food, makes the cells of your body reproduce younger cells instead of older cells.

The best auxinon foods I know of, says Mr. Landone, are found in mung bean sprouts.

Besides giving you this mysterious factor which makes youthful cells, sprouts also multiply vitamin E, vitamin C and all the B vitamins in the seed, and sprouts include vitamin K. They are of course very rich in zinc and all the other trace minerals. By all means, you should develop a sprouting habit. Keep a supply in your kitchen and you'll find your love life improving.

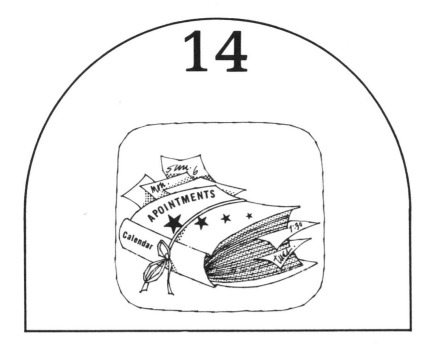

Your Lonely
Days Are Over!

Looking at Mirabelle Jansen, a wealthy, well-dressed, attractive woman, you might regard her with envy, as someone who has everything. You would never guess that her only weekend companion is a heavy heart.

"I simply dread Sundays," she confided to me one day when she came to the hospital where I was working for physiotherapy.

"People who have families around them don't seem to realize that for those of us who live alone, Sunday is the loneliest day of the week. It just seems to me that everybody in the world is busy with family dinners, family picnics or trips somewhere, and I am alone with nothing to do and no one to do it with. I feel so unnecessary, so unloved and rejected, that I actually have thoughts of suicide. I can stand the rest of the week, but Sundays are pure hell."

Loneliness, it has been shown, is a spur to mental depression and even to suicide, and it goes without saying that the lives of many older people are marked by deep-seated loneliness, brought on by living alone, eating alone, and separation from family or loss of dear ones.

Dr. Pearl Swanson, distinguished Illinois nutritionist, discloses a most interesting example. An alert, energetic 75 year-old woman was leading a busy life. She was employed, active in the affairs of the church, the Golden Age Group and other community projects. But she lived alone.

She ate regular meals that were of a quality suitable for the maintenance of good nutrition. But metabolism tests revealed that she suffered from severe nitrogen deficiency. Two years later she was observed again. Her grandson had come to live with her and though her meals furnished the same amount of protein as they had before, a marked change in its utilization occurred. Instead of losing nitrogen, she was retaining it. Companionship played a vital role in maintaining proper nutrition for this woman. And yet, one would scarcely have guessed that she had been lonely.

If this woman suffered from malnutrition because of loneliness even though she was eating well, how about the millions of oldsters living alone who never bother to prepare a decent meal for themselves? They are certainly courting a nutritional disaster.

184

If you do live alone, you should consider mealtime an important and exciting part of your day. Get yourself a new cookbook, preferably one that tells you how to prepare natural foods that contribute to health. Drool over the recipes and prepare them for yourself. Chances are you will be so excited about the aromas that are filling your home that you will want to find someone to share your meal with you. This is always a nice experience.

Plan a dinner for some friends—people you want to know better or people you like and want to share a pleasant time with. Find someone who is just as lonely as you are to share some meals with you, and you will be writing your name in the Book of Gold. You will find as a very nice dividend of this kind of gesture, that you will soon be invited into other homes because people do like to reciprocate.

Your days and evenings will be lightened and heightened by the preparations for these occasions, so that loneliness will have no opportunity to sneak into your heart. As guests come in your front door, loneliness slips out the back door.

Everyone has tremendous potential. Maybe you have writing talents you have always wanted to develop. Very likely a group of like-minded writers has already been organized in your community, a group which would welcome you, criticize your efforts in a friendly, helpful way and show you how to submit a manuscript for publication and for pay. Talk about fulfillment! I have seen many older people in my own writers' group read stories which they have worked on all week, and swell with pride as the group praised their efforts and suggested markets.

Their days were filled with hope as they mailed manuscripts. The mailman's visit was a time of excitement. Usually he brought rejection slips. But these were considered a mark of accomplishment, too. One woman saved hers optimistically. They were a testament to the fact that she was working at being a writer. She knew her efforts would pay off eventually. And—great day in the morning—the mailman did bring her a check from a publisher one day. The light in her eyes was multiplied by a thousand watts, and it's still glowing.

Needlework is another venture which can take the loneliness out of your evenings. Find a group associated with your YWCA, community center or your church who are interested in needlework—or start your own group. Get together for a good old-fashioned sewing bee, and keep the kettle on while your fingers fly and you share tales.

Another very good way of making Sunday the nicest day in the week, instead of the loneliest, is to volunteer as a Grey Lady at your local hospital and specify that you want to work on Sundays. They'll love you for it because Sunday workers are hard to get. Yet the care of patients continues every day of the week. One widow I know gave her Sundays to Grey Lady work for years and today she is considered the most valuable Grey Lady on the staff. Through her hospital work, she met a widowed physician who also was lonely on Sundays. You guessed it. They are now Dr. and Mrs. And

they both work at the hospital on Sundays.

Maybe Saturday night is the time when you feel the sharp pangs of loneliness, then volunteer your services for that evening. You're never lonely when you're rendering a service. You will find that the time you spend bringing a note of cheer and comfort to others will be reckoned as your finest hours.

If you tend to be overweight, handcraft hobbies can be your salvation. Dr. L. Melvin Elting, D.O., whose practice is limited to the treatment and control of obesity, says that "In the armamentarium used to combat this disease, one weapon must be designed to keep patients' hands and minds off of food. Many so called 'compulsive eaters' are not really bored with their surroundings; they eat out of habit, as a background to whatever they may be doing regardless of their interest in food."

To try to break this insidious pattern, Dr. Elting insists that his patients take up a hobby. Since the hands must be actively involved, handcrafts become the logical choice, and, says Dr. Elting, "Many of my formerly-fat patients have become happily involved in macrame, mosaics, wood-working, stained glass and, my own choice, metal working in brass or silver." (*Obesity-Bariatric Medicine,* Vol. 3., No. 1, 1974).

The rationale is that you are too involved in what you're doing to think of food, and your hands get grimy so you can't go to the refrigerator very easily. You kill two birds with one stone, your loneliness and your obesity. Dr. Elting reports that one patient, Larry Gargulio, lost 60 pounds after beginning treatment.

One of the best tickets I know of to a wonderful world without loneliness is hobbies. Do you remember how, in your younger, busier days, you thought how you would love to try your hand at watercolors, at pottery, at making those fantastic beaded flowers, at decoupage or at jewelry and crafting lovely candles? Well, now there's a time for everything under the sun. And now is the time for you to fill those lonely moments with any one of those absorbing interests. The Hobby Industry Association of America, at 200 Fifth Avenue, New York 10010, will be glad to send you a booklet which will open up the great big wonderful world of hobbies to you. You may be intrigued by rock collecting, botany, the study of insects and butterflies—every aspect of the world of nature is fair game for a hobby. If you are so inclined, such complex pursuits as electronics and chemistry or outdoor hobbies like model building make absorbing hobbies.

You make new friends when your horizons expand. The rapport among people who share the same hobby is beautiful.

"Happiness is never having to say, 'I have nothing to do'," says Lavonne Bunther in *Modern Maturity*, (February-March, 1974). "Too many lonely people," she says, "sit back and wait for the world to come to them. Friendship and contact with the busy world around us takes some effort." She suggests 16 ways to keep active and to add new dimensions to your life. One suggestion is to "keep a birthday file". Every day, like right after breakfast, when the lonely clouds begin to form, take a look at your birthday file, pull out the names of people with birthdays coming up and write a cheery little note. You will not only be spreading good feelings, you will be dispelling your blues.

Another excellent suggestion is to give a children's party. How long is it since you enjoyed the children in your neighborhood? Bake some good nutritious cookies and let the neighborhood children in for a non-birthday party, a la Alice in Wonderland. They will love you for it and ever afterwards they will greet you with an affection that will make your day glad.

If you don't have a cat or a dog, and your living quarters cannot accommodate one, try a bird for a pet. The pleasure of caring for another life will make your life more enjoyable.

By all means have a variety of plants on your windowsills. Plant herbs, like parsley, basil, oregano, marjoram, dill. The fragrance will tease your appetite. And they make wonderful additions to your salads.

Be a kitchen farmer and raise your own sprouts. Watching things grow gives a sense of renewal. Sprouts have so much to offer, they will nourish your body as well as your soul.

Get interested in food. People I know who have managed to acquire 80 years or more are people who have a keen interest in what they eat and how to prepare it. Even though they may eat alone, they make it their business to prepare three good meals every day.

Plan your meals ahead. Get excited about new dishes. Try not to repeat a food within the same week and do try to include something new several times a week. There is an old Japanese saying that every time you eat a food which you have never tasted before, you add 75 days to your life. Try avocados, mangoes, persimmons, buckwheat groats, millet or triticale (the new high protein grain that is the child of rye and wheat).

But, by far the nicest thing that you can do to brighten your life is something that will brighten the life of someone else. Learn to communicate with the deaf, for instance, or help to make talking books for the blind. If you have your hearing and your vision, you are indeed blessed.

Helen Keller who was both blind and deaf, said that "the problems of deafness are more complex, if not more important, than those of blindness. Deafness is a much worse misfortune because of the loss of the most vital stimulus—the sound of the human voice that brings language, sets thoughts astir, and helps us in the intellectual company of man."

In many communities classes are offered in sign language. They are usually held at one of the local hospitals in conjunction with the speech and hearing center. Take advantage of these classes and you will have an opportunity to communicate with the "silent minority." It might even lead to a meaningful career as an interpreter for the deaf.

Choose two or three of the suggestions I have offered

and you will soon be so busy, and so involved, that you will wonder where the loneliness went.

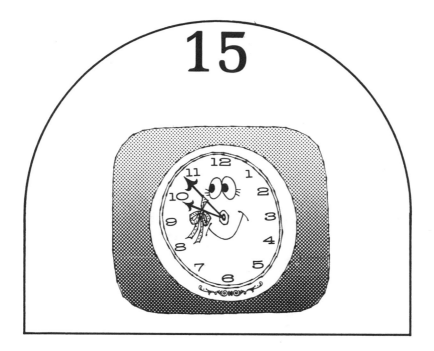

How to Stop
the Aging Clock

If we are to slow the aging clock as we add years to our lives, let's first understand what factors cause us to age, and what factors contribute to the glow of youth. Then we shall know where our enemies are, and how to avoid them, and where our friends are, and how to cultivate them.

First, we should realize one thing. No one ever dies of old-age. That's what Professor Hans Selye says in his excellent book, *The Stress of Life.* To die of old-age would mean that all the organs of the body would be worn out proportionately, from having been used too long. But this is never the case. We die because one vital part has worn out before the rest of the body. We grow old because we are unable to replace all of the parts that wear out as rapidly as they wear out, says Dr. Bernard Strehler, researcher in gerontology at the University of Southern California.

Aging begins when the DNA and RNA molecules (the only substances in the body which are capable of reproducing themselves) fail to reproduce exactly as before. This discrepancy in the reproduction of cells is so slight that it is not detected by the body's information sources. It works like this: As you age, so do your nucleic acids, which form your genetic patterns. These patterns become less distinct and the replication of cells is consequently less accurate. This slight deviation in replication of your cells can give rise to a host of problems. For example, it can cause reduction in the secretion of liver bile. A diminished supply of bile increases the likelihood of infection and decreases absorption of the fat soluble vitamins A, D, and E. As the liver becomes less efficient, there is less utilization of these vitamins and more excretion.

Benjamin S. Frank, M. D., in his book *Nucleic Acid Therapy in Aging and Degenerative Disease* (Psychological Library, 1969) demonstrates the importance of the nucleic acids DNA and RNA and related metabolites not only to a longer life free of degenerative disease, but to that wonderful quality of feeling young as long as you live.

Dr. Frank believes that the way to maintain youthfulness is to help your body's DNA and RNA renew themselves and keep their patterns of genetic information as clear and distinct as a new etching. In his experiments, he achieved phenomenal results by using a complete dietary

194

regimen rich in nucleic acids. On this dietary regime, patients began to shed some of the stigmata of old age; wrinkles in the forehead decreased in depth, there was a gradual decrease in size and pigmentation of lentigos (brownish pigmented spots) and of senile keratoses (horny wart-like growths), there was a lessening of dryness of the skin, a marked decrease of calluses on the feet, there was a more youthful gait and attitude, and the brain showed an increase in mental acuity.

The foods which are rich in nucleic acids are yeast, seafood of all kinds and organ meats. But chief among these foods is brewer's yeast. Dr. Frank has found that brewer's yeast, consumed in generous quantities, has an almost uncanny ability to recharge the batteries of the worn out cells, thus giving them a renewed capacity to create the mysterious condition that gives you the look and the feel of youth.

Dr. Frank also recommends desiccated liver, sweetbreads, small sardines and supplementary B vitamins and minerals. This diet supplies at least 30 milligrams a day of nucleic acids. (Two hundred milligrams of brewer's yeast would supply this amount.) In extreme cases, however, he recommends 300 milligrams a day.

The effects of Dr. Frank's regimen were sensational. Even on dosages as low as 30 milligrams daily, patients reported an increase in energy and a sense of well-being within a week. Patients who were taking the higher doses however, reported a new zest and vitality as early as the second or third day.

The effects were not only felt. They were visible, most noticeably on the skin of the face. The effect was almost as if an artist, with a loving brush, and a palette of rosey hues, came in the stealth of night and, with a puckish grin, touched up the canvas.

As the wrinkles decreased in depth there was an increase in the tightness and the moistness of the skin, as if the artist had also stripped ten years from the calendar.

It was not only the face that showed this remarkable effect. The skin at the elbows and knees became less rough. Most noticeably, the back of the hand improved in smoothness in most cases in three or four months.

These patients, though they enjoyed results which seemed magical, had merely taken five grains of nucleic acid daily, five days a week, for three months along with a therapeutic B complex capsule, both taken with lunch. A grain equals slightly more than 68 milligrams. Five brewer's yeast tablets of seven and a half grains each would provide five grains of nucleic acid.

If age can be estimated by appearance of the facial skin, then these patients decreased in age by ten years or more, Dr. Frank reports.

These patients became younger not only on the outside where it showed, but also on the inside where it was felt. The heart function of patients with coronary heart disease and congestive heart failure was clearly improved. Their electrocardiographs showed improvement and they also enjoyed

196

increased exercise tolerance.

The effects were not only physical. Patients who never could remember where they put their glasses or who it was who married who-cha-ma-call-it, began to recall events of yesterday and last week as well as the details of the ill-fated Lusitania's sinking.

In many older people there is a problem of degeneration of brain neurons and associated structures, plus diminished cerebral-vascular circulation. Since it was noted that circulation improved in other areas, it is reasonable to assume that cerebral circulation also benefited and more blood was getting to the brain.

We can assume that with the new influx of nutrients carried by the blood to the brain, that there is an improvement not only in memory but in a person's awareness and ability to think clearly. This leads to a new feeling of optimism, courage, and recovery of lost initiative. An interest in new activities follows and it has been shown that this helps you to live it up and live longer.

If brewer's yeast provided only nucleic acids to your diet, it would be enough to warrant its inclusion. But, brewer's yeast is a storehouse of many nutritional elements that help you to feel and look younger.

One of them is chromium which stimulates the activity of enzymes involved in energy metabolism. It is needed by the body in small amounts, but that little bit of chromium plays a big role in the health of your heart. Tissue taken from the bodies of persons killed by heart attacks tends to be deficient in chromium.

When researchers fed experimental mice or rats low chromium diets, the animals' growth rates were impaired. The inner walls of their blood vessels were pocked with fatty deposits like those that gradually clog the arteries and cause heart attacks in humans. Significantly, their ability to handle sugar was frequently so severely disturbed that blood sugar levels rose to a point where many of the animals excreted sugar in their urine. (One of the signs of diabetes). They died much sooner than animals who received even minute amounts of chromium in their drinking water.

Dr. Walter Mertz, chief of the department of biological chemistry at Walter Reed Army Institute of Research, points out that chromium also plays an important role in the synthesis of fatty acids and cholesterol in the liver, an early step in glucose metabolism (*Food and Nutrition,* December 1966).

But, here's the good news. Dr. Mertz found that impaired efficiency of glucose metabolism could be prevented "by adding a few percent of brewer's yeast, or of trace amounts of trivalent chromium to the diet. Moreover, the fully developed deficit could be cured by one oral dose of 20 micrograms or an intravenous injection of .1 microgram chromium in the form of certain complexes."

Does it work the same way on humans as it does on mice? It sure does. When supplements of chromium were given for 15 to 120 days, improved glucose tolerance was noted in four of six diabetics (*Science,* May 27, 1966). In

HOW TO STOP THE AGING CLOCK

another test reported in the same journal, five healthy male subjects aged 19 to 30 years received 100 grams of glucose by mouth after an overnight fast. When samples of blood were drawn immediately before and 30 minutes after administration of the glucose, there was a definite rise in plasma chromium in all five subjects, demonstrating that the body mobilizes its chromium forces to help handle excess sugar. If it does not have a supply of chromium, it cannot do the job.

However, only tiny amounts of inorganic salts of chromium are absorbed from the gastrointestinal tract when chromium supplements are given orally—probably only about .5 percent of the dose. Dr. Henry Schroeder, who has done considerable work with trace minerals, suggests that much larger percentages of naturally-occurring chromium complexes are absorbed from foods such as brewer's yeast.

Brewer's yeast helps in even more ways. As we get older our resistance to disease seems lower. The chest cold you got rid of in a few days when you were a mere youngster of 39 is much harder to shake off now. Infections and cuts don't heal so quickly as they used to.

At a seminar on "Nutrition and the Future of Man" held in 1971, Dr. A. E. Axelrod of Pittsburgh, pointed out that in order to produce the antibodies that fight against bacterial infections, we need three members of the B family that are scarce in our diets and frequently missing from the vitamin B supplements of the drugstore variety. They are pyridoxine (vitamin B6), folic acid and pantothenic acid.

Brewer's yeast gives you all three in good proportion and the odds are that if you take it, you will resist infections when you are 60 as well as you did when you were sixteen.

And that's not all you get from brewer's yeast. This smallest of all plants—about one four thousandth of an inch in diameter or about the size of a human blood corpuscle—contains all the elements of the vitamin B complex. In comparison with several other foods high in vitamin B, here's how brewer's yeast stands:

FOOD	PARTS OF VITAMIN B₁ PER 100 GRAMS
Brewer's yeast	5,000 to 8,000
Lean pork	300 to 750
Dried lima beans	450 to 600
Liver	300 to 420

FOOD	PARTS OF VITAMIN B₂ PER 100 GRAMS
Brewer's yeast	2,500 to 4,700
Lean pork	200
Dried lima beans	790
Liver	1,800 to 2,200

Over the centuries, since the days of the early Egyptians, yeast has been used for baking and for brewing. As more and more information has accumulated about the nature of yeast plants, the cultivation of them has developed into a major industry.

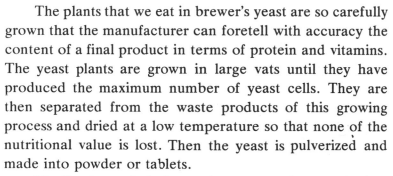

15

HOW TO STOP THE AGING CLOCK

The plants that we eat in brewer's yeast are so carefully grown that the manufacturer can foretell with accuracy the content of a final product in terms of protein and vitamins. The yeast plants are grown in large vats until they have produced the maximum number of yeast cells. They are then separated from the waste products of this growing process and dried at a low temperature so that none of the nutritional value is lost. Then the yeast is pulverized and made into powder or tablets.

The live bacteria in brewer's yeast are destroyed when the yeast is dried. It is not advisable to eat live (that is, baker's) yeast. The yeast plant needs large amounts of B vitamins to grow. Once inside your digestive tract, a yeast plant that is still alive can steal B vitamins from you. But, since brewer's yeast is no longer alive, you are able to benefit from all the B vitamins the plant stored up for itself.

Yeast is a rich source of high grade protein (protein containing all the essential amino acids). It is also rich in zinc, that mineral so important to the health of the prostate gland. Because yeast contains quite a lot of phosphorus, which must be balanced against your intake of calcium and magnesium, it's a good idea to supplement your diet with sources of these two important minerals. Bone meal and dolomite tablets will provide them. Or you can get yeast which comes supplemented with the balanced amounts of both calcium and magnesium.

Powdered yeast is preferable to flake yeast which has a lower vitamin content, weight for weight. One tablespoon of

201

powdered yeast is equivalent to five to nine tablespoons of the flakes. Yeast tablets are all right, but you need a heck of a lot of them. Ninety tablets are equivalent in mineral, protein and vitamin content to one heaping tablespoon of powdered yeast. Yeast, incidentally, is a great food for weight watchers. It contains almost no fat, starch, or sugar.

Some people say they just can't tolerate the flavor of yeast. If *you* feel that way, experiment. Try several varieties until you find the one which is palatable. The flavor is of course a matter of personal preference.

Adelle Davis suggests that the best way for a beginner to take yeast is to add no more than one teaspoon to a large glass of fruit juice and increase the amount very gradually as you become accustomed to it. One reason for taking yeast in small amounts at first is that, if your digestion is below par, yeast can cause gas. Ironically, faulty digestion usually results from a lack of B vitamins, so the more gas you get from yeast, the more deficient you may be in B vitamins, and the more you probably need the yeast.

Funny thing is you could eat sugar by the cup and get no gas because sugar couldn't support the growth of anything. Yeast, an excellent food, supports the growth of many things. If you lack hydrochloric acid in your stomach, or produce too few digestive enzymes, much of the yeast may remain undigested and your intestinal bacteria attack it with glee. That's where the gas comes from. On the other hand, if your digestive process is excellent, you will have no gas or feeling of fullness from taking yeast.

You can of course add yeast to soups, stews, casseroles, and many of the things you bake. But to insure a sufficient daily intake, I always take a yeast broth (two heaping tablespoons of powdered yeast in an eight-ounce cup of hot water), as a beverage instead of coffee or tea at break time. I spike it with a good vegetable seasoning powder. I may also add a teaspoon or two of an instant soup. Sometimes I add a half cup of sprouts and eat it with a spoon—like a good hearty soup. And sometimes I put a few chunks of cheese in the hot water and enjoy a delicious cheese soup while I get my B vitamins and nucleic acids.

Get started on brewer's yeast right away. Not only will you stop the aging clock, you might turn it back just a little bit.

On Carob Bananas,
Carrots and Grandchildren

I am usually just about five feet tall—on tiptoe. But on June 25, 1971, I was 10 feet tall. I did not hand out cigars (I don't like the smell) but I did hand out carob confections. "Just call me grandma," I said to everyone who crossed my path, "and may your day be as sweet as mine."

If you think you were excited and overcome with joy the day your first baby was born, just wait until you're a grandparent. There's nothing like it. A grandchild is a chance to see the world again—brand new. This time with a heart that has been well-seasoned.

Every grandma and grandpa loves the children of his children with an intensity that sometimes blots out good sense. We all want to be loved by the little tykes who pull

205

on our heart strings. We all want that big hug, that yelp of joy when the children see us arriving for a visit.

How do you win the love of your grandchildren? What do you take to them; what do you bake for them? How do you show your love? Grandparents who come laden with lollipops and sugar cookies as a token of love are really hurting their grandchildren.

Dentists will attest to the fact that the more grandparents a child has, the worse his teeth are likely to be.

Little Dianne was blessed with two sets of grandparents and four sets of great-grandparents. Her parents had their choice of babysitters who were eager to provide their services free. And they had sweets for their grandchild each time they saw her.

At the age of eight, little Dianne did not have a tooth in her mouth without a filling or a cavity. Her dentist said he had never seen so many bad teeth in so young a child.

In medical literature, there is the story of a child who made life miserable for his teacher—but only on Mondays. The rest of the week he was almost normal, but on Mondays he just couldn't sit still. His attention span was short and his antics were the kind that were driving his teacher up the radiator pipes.

The teacher learned that this child visited his grandparents every weekend. They doted on him and gave him everything they thought his tummy desired—cookies, lollipops, soda, gumdrops, and so forth. It was determined that the overload of sugar, plus the artificial flavorings and colors, made this child hyperactive (ants in his pants). Millions of children suffer from this syndrome. Not only are they failing in school, they are early candidates for diabetes, heart trouble, obesity, dermatitis, gout, and false teeth. I wonder how many of these children were started on this road by well-meaning, but misguided, grandparents.

There is a bubble gum machine near the door of the bank I go to. I see grandmothers, and mothers too, I must confess, come in with tots who always make a beeline for the multicolored balls in the big glass container and yell, "Can I have a penny, can I have a penny for chewin' gum?"

Everything in me silently screams, "No, no!" But apparently these folks aren't tuned in to my wavelength. The children get the pennies and fill their mouths with some of the worst, most poisonous looking junk ever concocted.

Don't be afraid to say "no" to your grandchildren. Believe me, you will not lose their love.

My doctor, a very wise man who was way ahead of his time and his profession, told me when my own kids were little, that if children never got a taste of sugar till the age of six, they would have fewer colds, fewer cavities, better dispositions, and would probably never develop a sweet tooth.

But every grandparent longs to indulge the children they love so much. "How can you refuse your grandchild when he asks for soda?" one grandmother asked me as her three-year-old grandson guzzled a bottle of Pepsi. Easy. You just don't have it in the house.

I remember how my kids were always delighted to come home to the smells that said "grandma is here"—how they loved the kugels, knishes and honey cakes that grandma made. These foods will always have an aura of love and caring about them for my children. I have learned how to prepare them so that they lose none of their wonderful nostalgic appeal and mouth-watering goodness but are also enriched with nutrients that help to bring the glow of health with every bite. That's what I call cooking with love and wheat germ.

If you really want to show your love, don't give your grandchildren lollipops. Give them carrot sticks. Bake goodies that will strengthen their teeth—not destroy them. I bake bone meal cookies for our granddaughter Jodi. She loves them.

When the hot summertime comes and other children are guzzling Icicles or Frostees, Jodi knows that there are ices for her in our freezer—made from fresh fruit juices. Or she may find a frozen banana coated with carob and coconut.

At the Farmers Market here in Allentown, there's a stand that features natural cheeses. When we stop there to buy some natural Muenster, the woman who runs the stand asks, "Are you going to see your granddaughter? Her other grandparents were here about half an hour ago. They bought cheese too."

But, you'll never guess Jodi's favorite thing. It's sprouts. When she's a little older I'm going to show her how to grow her own. There's a miracle in every little seed. What joy to see the wonder of it through the eyes of a child!

Children and grandparents have a very special relationship. They have a unique interest in and involvement with each other. The generation gap between grandparents and grandchildren is a very nice comfortable cushion. Helene Deutsch points out that "closeness to the next generation may interfere with the ability of adolescents to bring their problems, worries, and troubles to their parents, or even to parental figures; but they often can relate to adults older than their parents with greater ease." (*Pediatrics,* 1972).

The generations, once removed, can talk to each other with less emotional conflict. They may disagree, but they do so with a good deal of humor and mutual tolerance, respect and affection.

And grandparents need involvement and opportunities to pass on their own experiences. "Tell me a story, Gramp, about you when you were a little boy," a child will plead. Children love these stories, and grandparents love to tell them. It is a most effective way to transmit values, answer questions, and disburse wisdom from one generation to the one from which it is twice removed.

As Dr. Albert Solnit, Director of the Child Study Center of Yale University, points out, "Men and women in their 60's, 70's and 80's suffer a great loss of stimulation and satisfaction if their resources are not used. Their acceptance of life's gradual winding down is jeopardized. The loss can be devastating. Retirement or slowing down should be the beginning of another chapter, not the end of the book. Indeed, the book should never end. Replacement is one kind of immortality and continuity is another" (*Pediatrics*, December 1972). Grandchildren can be a source of this necessary stimulation.

I am reminded of the Talmudic tale of the old man who was busily digging a hole in which to plant a fig tree. A traveler passing by laughed at him and said, "Do you expect to live long enough to taste the fruit of this tree?"

"Tell me," the old man said, "did you ever taste a fig?"

Index

A

213

extremities, lower, blood circulation and, 44

F

fat(s), polyunsaturated, 119
　walking and, 50
feet, problems with, aging and, 43, 44
　vitamin E and, 45, 46
feminity, menopause and, 57
financial status, aging and, 28
flour, chromium and, 10
　manganese and, 11
　refined, body weight and, 13, 14
　whole-grain, foods containing, 14
fluorides, backaches and, 128
　rheumatoid spondylitis and, 128
folic acid, disease resistance and, 199
food, chewing of, importance of, 25, 26
fruit, constipation and, 23
fudge, carob nut, recipe for, 143

G

gangrene, diabetic, vitamin E and, 45
gardening, as exercise, 36
gardens, land for, 37, 38
gas, intestinal. See *intestinal gas.*
gifts, for patients in hospitals, 131-135, 143-146

gland(s). See also name of gland.
　arthritis and, 103, 104
　sex and, 177, 178
glucose, chromium and, 198
　hypoglycemia and, 150
grain, whole, manganese and, 11
grandchildren, relationship with, 205-210
Gray Ladies, as service project, 35
Green Thumb, 36, 37
gums, bioflavonoids and, 77
　bleeding, cause of, 77
　disease of, 70
　　calcium and, 76
　　diet and, 71
　inflammation of, causes of, 76
　pantothenic acid and, 73
　protein and, 77
　teeth and, 70
　vitamin C and, 77

H

halvah, recipe for, 143
handicrafts, as activity, 187
HCl. See *hydrochloric acid.*
health, importance of, 29, 30
　role of vitamin E in, 46
heart, care of, 109-120
　chromium and, 197
heart attacks, chromium and, 10, 197, 198
　oxygen supply and, 50
　sex and, 176
　walking and, 49-51
hobbies, as activity, 187, 188
hormone(s). See also name of hormone.

diet and, 67
female sex. See *estrogens.*
    menopause and, 58-61
    steroid, vitamin C and, 19
hospital, patient's rights in, 141
hot flashes, 55-68
    vitamin E and, 60
hydrochloric acid, aging and, 81
    arthritis and, 87
    body's production of, 91
    deficiency of, consequences of,
        86, 87
    prevalence of, 89, 90
    problems caused by, 81
    symptoms of, 88
    function of, 82, 83
    indigestion and, 85
    sugar and, 91
    turista and, 86
hypoglycemia, glucose and, 150
    psychiatry and, 149

I

ileus, pantothenic acid and, 95
indigestion, hydrochloric acid and,
    85
insomnia, nutrition and, 166, 167
intelligence, aging and, 28
intermittent claudication, 46
intestinal gas, brewer's yeast and,
    202
    causes of, 93
    heart pain and, 94
    pantothenic acid and, 94-96
iodine, source of, 178
    thyroid gland and, 62
iron, inorganic, vitamin E and, 64
irregularity. See *constipation.*

J

Jerusalem artichoke, blood sugar
    and, 26
jogging, walking and, 49

K

kelp, iodine and, 178

L

lactic acid, anxiety and, 163
lameness, 46
laxatives, dangers of, 22
lecithin, cholesterol and, 117-120
    daily requirement for, 119
    diabetics and, 26
    egg yolks and, 13
lemon juice, constipation and, 24
limping, 46
Little House, 39, 40
liver, aging and, 27
loneliness, activities to combat,
    185-191
longevity, daily behavior and, 34
    predictors of, 32, 33
lozenges, vitamin C, smoking and,
    34
lungs, walking and, 50
lupine beans, blood sugar and, 26

M

magnesium, deficiency of, results.

215

N

O

P

pain, from backache, relief of, 124-126
threshold of, vitamin B₁ and, 71, 72
pantothenic acid, daily requirement of, 97, 98
deficiency of, signs of, 73, 74
disease resistance and, 199
emotional stress and, 152
function of, 96, 97
gums and, 73
ileus and, 95
intestinal gas and, 94-96
mental attitude and, 151, 152
sleep and, 174
sources of, 75, 76, 98
surgery and, 95
tooth grinding and, 74, 75
paralytic ileus, pantothenic acid and, 95
parathyroid gland, calcium and, 66
parties, for children, as activity, 189
patients, gifts for, 131-135, 143-146
rights of, 141
peanut butter confections, recipe for, 144
peptic ulcers, theories about, 83
periodontal disease, 70
calcium and, 76
diet and, 71
pets, as activity, 189
physical exercise. See *exercise.*
physique, walking and, 50
pituitary gland, emotional stress and, 104
poker back, fluorides and, 128
polyunsaturated fatty acids, daily

requirement for, 119
posture, intestinal gas and, 93
potassium, necessity of, 11
sodium and, 169-171
white bread and, 11
protein, arthritis and, 106
deficiencies of, signs of, 12
gums and, 77
menopause and, 67
need for, 12
sources of, 12, 13
prunes, constipation and, 132
psychiatry, hypoglycemia and, 149
pulmonary embolisms, vitamins and, 136-138
pulse, lower extremities and, 44
pyridoxine. See *vitamin B₆.*

R

rheumatoid arthritis. See *arthritis.*
rheumatoid spondylitis, fluorides and, 128
riboflavin, deficiency of, signs of, 16
sources of, 16
Rinse's mash recipe, Dr., 116, 117
RNA, aging process and, 194
root-auxin, youth and, 181
rose hips, vitamin C and, 19

S

salad(s), constipation and, 24
salt, as stimulant, 167-169
foods containing, 170
schizophrenia, niacin and, 154

217

T

sources of, 15, 16, 72, 160
thrombosis, deep vein, causes of,
  135, 136
thyroid gland, emotional distress
  and, 103
  iodine and, 62, 178
  needs of, 62
  sex and, 178
  vitamin E and, 62
thyroid hormone, deficiency of,
  symptoms of, 61
tobacco, use of. See *smoking*.
tooth grinding, nutrition and,
  74, 75
tranquilizer, calcium as, 171-173
  vitamin B_6 as, 174
traveling, upset stomach and, 83, 84
turista, hydrochloric acid and, 86

U

ulcers, peptic, theories about, 83

V

vegetable oil, vitamin E and, 64
vision, blurred, smoking and, 34
vitamin(s). See also specific
  vitamin.
  alfalfa sprouts and, 134
  anti-stress. See *pantothenic
    acid*.
  importance of, 15-22
  pulmonary embolisms and,
    136-138
  sleep and, 174
vitamin A, effects of, 17

nucleic acids and, 27
old age and, 22
sources of, 17
vitamin B. See also specific B
  vitamin.
  sources of, 26
  types of, 15-17
vitamin B_1. See also *thiamin*.
  deficiency of, 71, 72
    signs of, 15
  pain threshold and, 71, 72
  sources of, 15, 16
vitamin B_2, deficiency of, signs of,
  16
  sources of, 16
vitamin B_3. See *niacin*.
vitamin B_6, as tranquilizer, 174
  deficiency of, signs of, 16, 17
  diabetics and, 26
  disease resistance and, 199
  sleep and, 174
  sources of, 17, 26
vitamin B_{12}, effects of, 17
  source of, 17
vitamin C, arthritis and, 106
  backaches and, 126-128
  body's use of, 19, 20
  cholesterol and, 113
  collagen and, 127
  deficiency of, signs of, 19
  detoxification and, 19
  gums and, 77
  pulmonary embolisms and,
    136
  scurvy and, 77
  sex glands and, 20
  sources of, 19
  steroid hormones and, 19
vitamin C lozenges, smoking and,
  34

vitamin D, deficiency of, signs of, 17, 18
  osteoarthritis and, 105
  sources of, 17
vitamin E, blood circulation and, 45-47, 64, 65
  deficiency of, effect of, 20
  diabetic gangrene and, 45
  estrogen and, 64
  feet and, 45, 46
  hot flashes and, 60
  iodine and, 178
  longevity and, 21, 22
  menopause and, 59, 60, 62-65
  mineral oil and, 64
  oxygen supply and, 47
  pulmonary embolisms and, 137, 138
  sex and, 177-179
  sources of, 20, 22, 65
  thyroid gland and, 62
  vegetable oil and, 64
vitamin K, sources of, 133, 134
  surgery and, 133

W

walking, benefits of, 48-54
water, community, acid deficiency and, 90

constipation and, 23
wealth, aging and, 28
weight, excessive, arthritis and, 105
  loss of, walking and, 50, 53
  refined flour and, 13, 14
  smoking and, 35
weight gain, smoking and, 35
wheat bran, cancer and, 12
wheat germ, uses of, 11
white bread, food value of, 10, 11
whole grain, manganese and, 11
whole-grain flour, foods containing, 14
writing, as activity, 185

Y

yeast, brewer's. See *brewer's yeast.*
yogurt, constipation and, 24, 25
  protein and, 13

Z

zinc, deficiency of, causes of, 179
  sex and, 179
  sources of, 179